LET THE POWER BE WITH YOU

LET THE POWER BE WITH YOU

EMPOWER YOUR THOUGHTS
EMPOWER YOUR LIFE

SHIVI DUA

wisdom tree

First published 2009
Reprinted 2010, 2012, 2015

ISBN 978-81-8328-149-2

Published by
Wisdom Tree
4779/23, Ansari Road
Darya Ganj, New Delhi-110002
Ph.: 23247966/67/68
wisdomtreebooks@gmail.com

Printed in India

CONTENTS

PREFACE

As a healer I come across people facing various types of problems — physical, mental, emotional, etc. Each problem that they face is unique in a way, but it has one common thread — each one stems from a set of negative beliefs carried by the person.

During each healing session with a client, though the healing is done at the soul level, the counselling at his conscious level is aimed at making him realise how he shapes up his life's events and contributes in creating his own stress. This always gives him a different perspective to look at his life and helps him to alter its course. He feels de-stressed instantly as he realises his own power and its potential to turn things around in his life.

At times those receiving healings from me have told me that the words they heard were precious and should have been recorded, when I was only speaking spontaneously what I believed in and felt the person needed to know, depending upon his particular needs.

Slowly thus, the idea emerged in my mind, of writing a book wherein I would bring forth what I understand about the power each individual inherently has to create a life of his choice for himself. This is the power I have realised within myself and by bringing my awareness to it, created peace within. As we get rid of the baggage of all the negative beliefs we had been living with, instantaneous manifestation of anything we want becomes a reality. The examples I have used throughout the book to illustrate my point are all from the real world. Some of them are from my own life.

Once we are at peace within ourselves, it reflects in every aspect of our lives. The book is intended for anyone who wants to create peace and harmony within oneself and improve his life, to be able to enjoy it to the full.

The book has been divided into five sections. The first one aims at understanding how a human being himself is responsible for everything that he experiences in his life. It explains the significance of the human thought patterns, how they are created, how they influence us and therefore how they can be used to influence us in a positive manner.

The second section deals with the various types of inner conflicts that weaken our own power to manifest whatever we want in life. It explains how we can resolve these inner conflicts and regain our inherent power to create a beautiful life for ourselves.

The third section deals with the various types of negative emotions that mar the relationships that are so important to us. By eliminating those negative emotions from the root, we can empower our relationships to be supportive for us rather than being blocks in our progress.

Our physical body reflects the stress we carry, in the form of pains, injuries and various ailments. By reclaiming our power we can naturally restore health to our physical body. This is explained in the fourth section.

The fifth and the last section explains how, having cleared all the blocks within ourselves at various levels, we can use our power to achieve what gives us the utmost satisfaction, which could be different for each individual.

The sixth section is a sum up of the various processes and healing techniques I have used over the years. Using these methods, I have been able to uncover my connection with my inner being as well as with the Creator. It might contribute in a small way, helping the readers similarly to find their inner power and use it to heal their lives.

I have often used the term 'the Creator' in this book. It refers to the creative force behind all creation, and not to any deity. It is the formless, shapeless energy source; the source of all that is, the supreme power that is above everything else. That is what I refer to even when I use the term 'God'.

During the healing sessions I connect with the cosmic energy which is the universal source of all knowledge. Many people have accessed this knowledge before me and as the energies of the planet are fast rising, more and more of us will find ourselves connected to the Divine. This book is an attempt to share with the readers, my perspective of a part of this universal knowledge.

May we all be blessed to lead our beautiful lives in the knowledge of the Creator and His boundless love for us.

SECTION I

KNOW YOUR POWER

Chapter 1

INTERNAL CONFLICTS

If I really am powerful,
where is my power and why is it hidden?

It is the ongoing internal conflict within us that keeps our power hidden. In fact, it may be said that we have been using this power ignorantly to create conflicts within us. These, in turn, have created stress for us at work, in relationships, in physical body, etc.

Our basic nature is to find peace and happiness. At the same time, over the years we have conditioned ourselves to give energy to all that is negative. Hence, this inner desire for peace and happiness is forever in conflict with the negative beliefs we have created within us over lifetimes.

Once you understand how it is the powerful you that created these internal conflicts for yourself, you will be able to create a different life for yourself — one that naturally provides you happiness.

From the age we, as children, start going to school, to our working lives, till our retirement, we live with stress and have to learn to keep it under check in order to be able to live life fully. This takes up a lot of our energy. Where does all this stress come from? Is it coming from the competition with the fellow students to score higher than them? From the undeserving colleague's promotion that came even before ours? From the relative who said something to us that he shouldn't have? The list is endless. All of it seems to be coming from various sources around us, and yet it actually emerges only from within us. Anything outside us can trigger stress in us only if there is a conflict inside us that resonates with it.

When a child begins school, it is introduced as a place where he will receive knowledge and learning that will one day help him become a successful person. Every child takes to this concept enthusiastically and begins enjoying learning. Very soon, though, all the elders around the child begin shifting their focus from the child's knowledge gaining to his score-card, and there begins a stressful school journey of the child. If our trust is firmly placed in the Creator and ourselves, our focus at our work place would be on doing our job to our satisfaction and not on what our various colleagues are achieving.

Each one of us (including each one around us) is on our own individual journey and any change that we can bring about is only in our own selves. Recognising and resolving our inner conflicts is what will bring peace inside us naturally.

In order to bring about any change within, we need to observe and understand ourselves. For this we need to devote some time to ourselves on a regular basis. If we make it a habit to be in solitude for sometime everyday, even if for a few minutes and observe our thoughts as they emerge, gradually we will form a habit of doing so even in the midst of our daily routine. Once we know what our negative thoughts are, we can then analyse them and train ourselves to think positively.

Each one of us is a powerhouse of energy and each thought that emanates from us is a power packet. It is very important to understand the significance of these power packets we create all the time because it is through these that we design our lives.

In the following chapters of this book, we will understand how these power packets are created and how they govern our lives. Further, we will look into some thought patterns that give rise to our inner conflicts. We will then see how, by identifying our negative beliefs and replacing them with the corresponding positive ones, we can get rid of our inner conflicts. We thus, eliminate stress from our lives, rather than having to manage it.

It is then that we naturally and easily get our vitality back and we achieve everything that we want to, effortlessly!

Chapter 2

THOUGHTS, THE POWER PACKETS

Aren't many of our thoughts just useless?

Each thought is a prayer and every prayer is answered. So, watch your thoughts!

Each thought germinating within us creates certain vibrations within and around us thereby reaching the Omnipresent naturally. We really do not need to make any effort to have our prayers heard or answered. Each prayer is answered as soon as it is heard and each prayer is heard as soon as it is said. The effort that we do need to make however, is in ensuring that *all* our thoughts are positive so that our prayers do not keep cancelling each others' effects.

I would like to use the term 'power packets' for thoughts because we give immense energy to the things we think about, through them. We have a source of a ceaseless flow of energy within us. That is our connection with the universal creative force which we often refer to as the Creator or God.

Everything that we think about receives this energy through our thoughts. When we accept our power, we also learn to send our power packets to the things/people/situations that give us happiness. We stop sending them to those that upset us because we don't want to energise them and increase their role in our lives.

At times, when we are praying, we might be asking the Creator to help us forgive those who have done us wrong while at other times we might be busy condemning the person for doing the same. Brooding over the past in this manner will give rise to anger within which will generate the feeling of revenge. In our ignorance, we are sending our power packets to the wrong that we experienced, the person we believe wronged us and the emotions of anger and revenge. These will then easily negate those we sent during our prayer for forgiveness. Later, we might even find it convenient to blame the Creator for not answering our prayers.

Accepting the past and whatever unpleasant may have taken place helps us integrate it within us. Reminding ourselves that the other person in question is entitled to his own way of looking at things and handling his life, helps us accept whatever happened between him and us in a neutral manner and move on. Only then we can continue to create positive vibrations within us of 'forgive and forget'. Actually it really should be 'accept and forgive'. Accept them as they are and forgiveness follows naturally. Trying to forget only makes us remember it some other time. Accepting it actually frees us of the burden.

Money is a basic necessity of life. Many prayers of most of us are about receiving more wealth, or at least enough for us to comfortably meet our needs. At the same time we associate a lot of negative energy with this entity. Money is often called a necessary 'evil'. It is believed to corrupt. So while we pray to be blessed with more wealth at many other times we might very innocently be telling the Almighty that if money does to people what it did to so and so, we are better off without it. In the process of judging people and situations that we experience, we lose the right perspective and develop negative beliefs, which then govern the future course of our lives.

It is the conflict within our thoughts that creates conflict in our lives that in turn creates stress for us.

Since each thought is a prayer that is answered, having conflicting thoughts like 'I must trust my accountant for he is a professional' and 'it is unsafe to trust anyone' has the potential to create a situation where you entrust your accountant with certain important responsibilities regarding finances and one fine day discover that a major fraud has been committed by him.

It was about four months since we had moved to Chandigarh when one morning on my daughter's way to school, her bus met with an accident. A truck banged against the bus and a window pane broke and fell on my daughter's hands giving her cuts and scratches at many places. While narrating the incident, she also told me that all the children in the bus were concerned about her. She said despite the blood and the pain, she felt nice as she got a reason to communicate with them. Even as she was saying this, she was reminded of similar events that happened with her at the different places we had lived in earlier. At that time too, it was through some sort of suffering that she got to make friends in her new school. She finally ended the narration with, "I knew something like this will happen and I will make friends here also." Needless to say, I pointed out to her that it was this belief of hers that was creating this misery for her time and again and that she deserved to make friends wherever she went easily and effortlessly.

In order to change our thought patterns, all we really need to do is watch them. Fighting or curbing our natural thought pattern only creates resistance within us to the natural flow of energy within us. Observe the stressful situation in your life and observe your thoughts relating to that. With some practice, you will be able to identify the set of negative thoughts that created the situation in your life. All you have to do then, is ask yourself how you would like your life to be in that particular aspect and what thoughts will create it for you. All that remains to be done next is to believe in your power to create your life afresh and send the right power packets out to the Universe.

Chapter 3

SUBCONSCIOUS, THE ENIGMATIC

How does it matter anyway,
what my subconscious carries?

Whatever we have in life today, the joys, the sorrows, the abundance, the dearth, the situations, the friends and relatives, is what we have been creating for ourselves over centuries. That's how long most of us have been on the planet! It is our own beliefs that govern the situations in our lives by drawing certain kinds of people towards us, making us act in a certain manner, etc. These beliefs have been developed over time, through our experiences. They are the lessons we learnt as a result of those experiences. The lessons learnt by us during the current lifetime remain with us as our conscious beliefs. Many of them seep through to the subconscious. Those learnt by us over the past lifetimes remain with our soul as the subconscious beliefs. These belief systems give rise to the thoughts in our mind.

The Creator of the Universe is an omnipotent, omnipresent

energy all around us and within us. Each thought arising out of us is like a command this energy carries out just as soon as it is created. Thus it is true that the energies of the entire Universe are ever ready to do whatever is required to make all our wishes come true. Only, we need to be sure of what it is that we are asking for. Very often we carry conflicting beliefs which lead to conflicting situations in our lives that give us stress. Once we start the process of introspection, identification and elimination of the negative thought patterns, we are left with only the positive ones and actually start experiencing instantaneous manifestation of our wishes.

Once I decided I wanted a new purse, I received one as a present within the next couple of days. Another time, I thought I was really bored of a particular pair of shoes I had and by that very evening both the shoes were in such a bad shape that I had to throw them away. These are the most trivial of the manifestations in day-to-day life that not just me but many of us may have experienced, but they point to the potential in us to create in our lives whatever we want. Physical manifestation of all our big and small wishes is a reality we are meant to experience. As we keep getting rid of our negative beliefs one by one, we begin experiencing it as the most natural way of life, which it is!

There is a lot of baggage our soul carries from its past experiences. We don't remember our experiences from our past lifetimes, but they have created their impact on the soul. At the time of a particular experience, we learn our lesson based on our intelligence and stage of evolution at that time. This lesson then stays in our subconscious for a long time, until something happens to change it. As long as it stays in our subconscious, it works constantly in such a way that we are either saved of a similar experience if it was a bad one or are benefited in that manner repeatedly if it was a good one. For example, if a person whom we greatly relied upon deceived us, we might be so shocked that rather than learning our lesson to be more discerning in trusting, we might develop the belief that it is unsafe to trust anyone. This belief then, in its own way of protecting us from being cheated further, will bring to us one untrustworthy person after another till we consciously understand the message that it is unsafe to trust. Yet we might not realise during all this suffering that it was our own reaction to an event that actually created further misery for us. Similarly if we, at some point of time, are greatly helped by our friends in some situation, we are likely to develop a belief that friends are always good and easy to find. Through this, we will create the blessing of many dependable friends for ourselves for many lifetimes.

We live our day-to-day lives thinking with our conscious mind. The mind is a very useful tool given to us by the Almighty. It should ideally be *used* when we need it such as to make choices or take decisions but we end up giving it full power to rule us and even to use us. In this process, we live our lives quite disconnected with our own higher selves, which in fact has a broader and higher perspective to our lives. We, therefore, have no access to our subconscious and it constantly stays with us as an enigma. For this reason, the subconscious beliefs gain more power than the conscious beliefs as the latter keep varying with experiences of new kind of events in life, whereas the former remain constant.

We might be unaware of what is there in our subconscious mind, but it constantly presents itself in our lives.

If we look back at our lives, there are certain patterns of situations that would be evident. Some are good, e.g. a person could be bestowed with a good amount of wealth throughout his lifetime or someone could be blessed with the constant love and support of near and dear ones. Some of them could be unpleasant like a person could face an inability to express his thoughts effectively, often leading to misunderstandings or someone might face rejection by friends/family. These patterns are indicative of positive/negative beliefs held in our subconscious.

Having realised what kind of negative beliefs our subconscious holds, we can begin our efforts to change those to the corresponding positive ones. Using repeated positive affirmations is one way of doing it. Reiki and Theta healing do it the energy way. Irrespective of how we do it, it certainly alleviates a lot of stress from within us. The need here is to understand the fact that there is much more to ourselves than what we see in the mirror. The physical body and the conscious mind simply are tools we are blessed with in order to carry out what is needed, so that our soul's aspiration is achieved, so that our higher self moves ahead on its path. If we begin to look at our lives objectively, as if from a distance, even if for a few minutes daily, we can easily identify and realise our true selves and our highest aspiration. Everything else is like the various accessories in a caravan; the vehicle being our physical body and the traveller in the vehicle our higher self. Understanding our true selves thus brings peace within. Once we are at peace within ourselves, nothing from outside can disturb us.

We are energy. Everything in this Universe is. The entire Universe is constituted only of energy, in various forms. Our eyes are trained to see certain forms. Other energy forms are invisible to our eyes, but they still exist. Some people train their eyes to see energy forms like the aura of an individual. The fact that the aura each human being has is not visible to most of us doesn't mean it doesn't exist. Each thought is also a powerful energy wave. So when we think about something, we give it energy. It is, therefore, important for us to remember that once we have identified a negative belief residing in us, we have to stop giving it energy and stop thinking about the negative events it created for us. Instead, we have to give energy to the corresponding positive belief.

Chapter 4

LAW OF KARMA

Oh, you mean I am suffering today
because I was bad in the past?

It is usually only when we suffer in some way that we turn towards spiritualism and stumble upon the term 'karma'. One of the first things we then learn is that if our karma is good, we are rewarded and if our karma is bad, we suffer miseries of varying intensities. We find it hard to accept that we could have been involved in something so bad that we should be paying thus. It is also difficult to adjust to the fact that we should be paying for something we don't even remember having done.

If we look at our current lifetime as a short phase in the very long journey of our soul, we will be able to understand our life better.

Our karma is how we respond to a situation/person/remark, etc. through our action, speech or thought. If we observe that the behaviour of a relative of ours who has recently become rich, changed towards us for the worse, we could either understand it as that individual's choice (in other words *his karma*) or develop a generalised belief that money spoils people. Only, in the latter case, we will start blocking money from flowing into our lives because we will associate a negative belief with money. Let us consider another man who is guilty of infidelity in marriage. His guilt might give him a belief that he is unworthy of a healthy relationship with his spouse. This belief will then create an unhappy marriage for him life after life. This is how our karma creates our destiny.

Karma is often perceived as God's punishment. "If I do wrong, God will punish me for it." This is a very common belief and creates in us a fear of God. Another term for being conscientious is being 'God-fearing'.

God is nothing but pure unconditional love. Whatever we might do, He is always there for us, loving and supporting us. His love never ceases for us, it never even becomes any less for any one of us. He loves us so much that He has put a part of Himself in each one of us giving us that power of creation! We are co-creating our lives with Him all the time, through our thoughts, words and actions. Therefore, by believing that God punishes and is an entity that needs to be feared, we actually keep God's grace away from us. If the Creator receives a message from us (in the form of our thought) that we are afraid of Him, He lovingly keeps away from us lest He frightens us.

Just like whatever wrong a child might do, his parents cannot have anything but love for him, God is our true parent, our Creator. Every household has certain rules of discipline and certain kinds of punishments, which are designed to teach the child the parents' perspective of the best way of living life. It is the job of the parents to keep the child on the right track, so that he makes the best out of his life. Similarly, in the Creator's Universe there are certain laws that govern us. One of them is the law of karma. It is through this law that positive/negative (as appropriate) rewards for our deeds are given to us.

Actually, even our karma has been created by our own selves. That is how powerful the Creator has made us. If we would live each breath of ours in consciousness and not sleepwalk through life, we can create an amazing life, an amazing world for ourselves! If only we would stop treating ourselves as hapless victims of the world and the situations around us, we could actually turn our lives into a series of wonderful experiences.

To understand and accept that it is we who have chosen to be in the circumstances that we are in, is the first step in changing things in our favour. To be able to change something, we need to accept two things. One, the thing/situation as it is. Two, the power we have to change it. By denying or running away from a situation, we only make it persist.

Take, for example, a situation where a person seems like an enemy to us because he seems to be doing everything that is against our good. We tend to look at such a person as a villain and ourselves as the hero. Actually villains exist only in movies. There really is no villain that Creator ever created. He created everyone equal, with the same creative energy and continues to bless everyone with the same unconditional love forever. It helps to remind ourselves at such times that it is we who, through our beliefs, have created this situation around us of which the other person is a part. He is also living his own karma and is trapped in his own set of beliefs. Negative energies like anger and revenge only prolong our suffering. It is only positive energies like compassion and forgiveness that can bring the situation to any kind of completion. Deep-rooted anger and vengeance against a person can actually make us suffer for many lifetimes, where we end up getting entangled in difficult situations with the same soul over and over again.

Ironically, it is common to have such a love-hate relationship amongst brothers who share a business and also a tussle for authority. The love for the other is there so they can't let go of the other, can't be indifferent to the other. Yet the egos they have built around their vulnerable self permit only the emotions of hatred and vengeance to be expressed.

Thus it is our karma created by ourselves that brings to us punishments or rewards for our deeds. God only loves us as we are.

We are creating our destiny each moment, through what we think, speak and act. That is our karma. We can never avoid karma. We are in it all the time. We can watch it so that we credit our karma account with more positive than negative, to begin with. We are living our past karma. Our destiny is constantly being created/changed by our present karma. We are presented with options each moment in our lives. The choices we make are our karma and decide our destiny.

Thus, our lives are dictated by none other than we ourselves, through our karma!

SECTION II

USE YOUR POWER

Chapter 5

ACCEPT WHAT IS

But don't I already?

Once we understand that it is our own selves, that has created the situations we are in and has drawn to us the people that are around us and has even made us as what we are, it should become very easy to accept the situations and the people around us. At times it doesn't because we, at our conscious level, want something better. It is important to understand two things here: one, it is very much possible to get that 'something better' which we want and we surely deserve it too, but only by accepting what we already have. Two, the best way for us to reach that 'something better' really was through what is there in the present. Our higher self had considered it necessary to experience certain things and learn certain lessons during this lifetime. So it created these situations for us. It is only by accepting the present moment in our full awareness, that we can have those necessary experiences and learn those essential lessons for our evolution. By denying the present moment and running away from the current situations, we not only increase our suffering, but also delay our evolution.

'Acceptance', therefore, is of utmost importance in our lives. When there are people/situations in our lives that we don't like, by accepting them we can actually save ourselves from a lot of misery. At times it seems difficult to do so. What we don't like in our lives, we tend to deny it, little realising that this attitude actually makes the situation persist, even worsen. Once we accept the presence of an unpleasant situation, just as we would a pleasant one, we have already begun the process of resolving it. Once we acknowledge a problem, our awareness shifts to finding a solution for the same. Hence, instead of the problem we start sending our power packets to finding the solution. Since we are constantly working with the Creator through our thoughts, the moment we ask for a solution, we are presented with one. When the universal creative force gives us something, it could be through another person, through a book or an idea that flashes in our mind; the ways are endless. We should be present in the moment, every moment, to be able to receive it.

Passive acceptance, means accepting something we don't like with a sense of dejection. It involves passively living a situation that we don't really enjoy thereby stagnating us. It might eliminate stress to a certain extent, but it doesn't remove the misery from our lives. Active acceptance on the other hand, i.e. accepting with our awareness focussed on changing things for the better and living the situation while consciously working at improving it helps us evolve and eventually brings joy to our lives.

Consider a man who works as a manager in a company. He is a sincere and capable employee. During a particular assessment year, he worked hard to bring about certain basic changes in the functioning of his department which contributed to the company's growth in a remarkable way. His work was even being acknowledged by his colleagues and the boss verbally. He felt a good promotion that year was certain. However, the promotion actually went to another peer of his. Now there could be three ways for him to react:

- Complete shock and despair. Feeling let down. Losing the enthusiasm in his work and in fact retaliating by bringing down the quality of work he puts into his job.
- Immediate resignation from his current job with the company.
- Initial shock and despair followed by accepting the situation with grace. He, then, gets back to his normal work routine, this time being more aware of his thoughts, watching out for any negative patterns that might be creating blocks in the way of achieving his goals and correcting them then and there.

The first type of reaction involves blame. He blames the company for doing him injustice. He wants to avenge the same. Blame is a negative energy. Once he brings down the quality of his work, he is sure to hate himself for it, leading to some more negative energy in the form of guilt. Besides, his low-grade work in the present is not something that he can use to bring the employer's attention to the high quality work that he did in the past. So, he invites only criticism, not acclaim. Thus, one type of negative energy leads to another and so on. Immediate resignation may be followed by a delay in getting another job or not getting the one most appropriate for him immediately. This would lead to frustration. Besides, wherever he might start working, the beliefs that created the situation for him in the first place are likely to do the same again.

Hence the best course to follow is the third one. Spending too much energy on what has happened never helps, especially if it was unpleasant. Learning our lesson and moving on to experience the beauty of life that lies ahead is what makes our life a wonderful journey.

Let us take another real life story. A friend of mine had little idea what her life would be like ten years hence when she completed her MBA and started working with a leading organisation. She got married and continued growing in her career too. She was working as the Manager Corporate Relations when her husband got posted in another city. As the family relocated, this lady's life changed drastically. She didn't have her in-laws living with her in the new city, so she had to shoulder the entire responsibility of taking care of her young son, which meant no full-time job for her. As luck would have it, she was unable to find a suitable part time occupation for herself in the new location.

She started feeling miserable, blaming her husband for the situation where she had to compromise on her career. She was so upset that she started cursing herself for getting married in the first place. Needless to say, the family life was anything but harmonious. When she got in touch with me and as we started having discussions about the current situation in her life, she learnt about acceptance. Slowly she began realising that she might not have expected this turn of events in her life but she really had nothing to complain. She had a husband who really cared about her and their son and had a good job. She had a son who was adorable. In fact, in those impressionable growing years of their son, it was best for her to devote more time to his upbringing. Once she accepted the situation as a passing phase and that it had come about at the right time as well as in the best possible way, she could see how beautiful her life truly was. Life naturally became enjoyable for her. The family bonding improved, too.

She is still holding onto her dream of being able to pursue her career again, but without any negativity attached to it.

SELF-ACCEPTANCE

The first step in accepting things as they are around us is to accept ourselves completely, unconditionally. Surprising as it might sound, one thing that we all tend to have the least acceptance for is the self. We tend to be most critical of ourselves. When we like someone, we compare ourselves with that person and find ourselves falling short of our expectations. This process goes on inside us all the time, sometimes even without our being aware of it.

A lady who was a professional and also managed a home and family went to a colleague's house for dinner. She was impressed with the way colleague's wife kept her house and conducted the entire dinner. During a conversation with the hostess, she complained that she never found enough time to similarly cook an elaborate meal and wished she also had the time to decorate her house. Such statements were a result of the internal process of comparison, judgement and self-defence that went on inside her during the dinner. So, instead of enjoying the beauty of the well-done house and the sumptuous dinner, she felt miserable as she was passing judgement about herself that she didn't match up to the hostess in a certain aspect of life. The most interesting part was that the hostess actually harboured a complex inside her that this particular colleague of her husband was a superwoman, managing home and work so well, whereas she was simply looking after her family.

No doubt there is always a room for improvement in each one of us. However, we should change ourselves with the positive attitude of bringing within us a quality that we love and appreciate, not because we are imperfect without it, because we aren't. When we accept ourselves completely just as we are, the change we want to bring about in ourselves happens naturally and effortlessly!

If the Creator of the Universe loves us the way we are, why can't we accept ourselves too? At times we do things expecting specific results. If the results, however, fall short of our expectations we like to call it our mistake. We internally keep condemning ourselves for having made that mistake for it kept our desired result away from us despite all our efforts. At such times, we are overlooking the learning that experience had to offer us. We must remember that what we got as a result was what we had, consciously or through the subconscious, sent our power packets to. So, we need to bring our awareness to those erroneously sent power packets and start sending them in the right direction. Developing guilt for whatever has happened in the past takes us away from ourselves. We did what we thought was right for us to do at that point of time. By remaining in denial about what happened and regretting it intensely we only keep sending our power packets to what we are unhappy about. Accepting it as our learning experience helps us move on to better experiences.

FILTERS

What we actually hear/see/feel in the world around us is actually held within us at conscious or subconscious level. (This fact can also be used to receive guidance about what the negative beliefs held in our subconscious are.)

This thing first struck me when about twelve years ago I went to the market for the first time after my daughter's birth. I was surprised to see the number of shops that marketplace had that sold children's clothes and toys. I had been to that place innumerable times before that but had never observed those shops. Obviously, they had not suddenly popped up out of nowhere. It was just that children's stuff was never the focus of my mind earlier.

As discussed earlier our subconscious beliefs govern our lives, life after life. I know a person who carries the belief that he shouldn't get married because it will never bring him happiness. It stems from the very deep impact which was possibly created by a marriage he was in that had left him miserable. In this lifetime, he keeps pointing at all the unsuccessful marriages around him. The numerous happy marriages around him, including his parents', fail to influence him. This is how we see/hear/feel through our own filters.

Hence if we believe that we are imperfect and need to perfect ourselves in certain areas in order to be loved and accepted, we are inviting criticism from others and not vice versa. If we lack confidence in ourselves, our 'energy body' conveys it and we always find it difficult to gain the confidence of others. We always desire to be perfect in everything, oblivious of the fact that there is no finishing line for the race of perfection. In other words, we really are perfect just as we are.

This process of passing judgement is further extended to others, e.g. *x* is very mean or *y* is very insensitive. Such remarks actually reflect our own hidden complexes. If we are unable to accept our own selves completely, how would we ever accept anyone else unconditionally? By not accepting people or things as they are, what are we achieving anyway?

Whatever is, just is, as it is! It doesn't cease to exist if we don't accept it. It wouldn't change simply because we don't like it the way it is.

Chapter 6

SURRENDER IS SELF-EMPOWERMENT

But doesn't surrender mean giving up?

Well, maybe in the dictionary it does, but don't we give up only when we realise that despite all our efforts we can't do it our way any more? Don't we give up only when we realise that there is someone or something more powerful than us? Doesn't giving up at that point instantly end the stress we had been living through? Well, then, why not surrender to the Almighty? Going a step further, why wait for ourselves to feel helpless before we surrender to the Creator?

By 'surrendering to the Creator', I mean realising that it is the universal creative force that has created all creation that really runs or maintains the entire creation, and in the highest and the best way. Yet He does for us only what we want Him to do, if we allow Him to. When we do a certain job, we do it within our own (self-created) limitations. When we allow *Him* to do the same, He does it in the best possible way.

A friend of mine once responded to the concept of 'surrender to Creator' by saying, "It is my life and I want to run it my way. So, if I just leave it to God, I might not get the results at work that I am aiming for. After all, I have to work for it. I can't get things without working for them."

By leaving it to Him doesn't mean inactivity on our part. Activity is inevitable. **When we leave it to the Creator, we allow the divine activity to take place through and around ourselves.** When we 'surrender' ourselves to Him, we allow a free flow of the divine energy through us, and then it is this divine energy that carries out the activity. So while what we want is being carried out without any effort on our part, we are even being energised as the divine energy flows through us. On the other hand, when we believe it is we who have to and must do everything in our lives, we not only apply all our efforts in doing those things, but also feel drained at the end of it.

A lady working with one of the leading airline companies felt harassed in life as her day began with making sure the first two meals for her family were prepared and ready, then packed her daughter off to school before she left for work at 7:30 every morning. When she reached home at eight every evening after a long, busy day at work, she had to prepare dinner for the family, end the day on time so as to be able to wake up fresh next morning and go through the same grind all over again. The grudges of not being supported by anyone kept her miserable. Once she learnt the concepts of trusting the Creator and surrendering to Him, she actually felt energetic even at the end of the day. The only change she has made in herself is to entrust God with carrying out all responsibilities for her, with a complete surrender of herself and her life to Him.

Whatever we want in our lives, whether it is a long-term

objective or things that we want in our day-to-day life, all we need to do is just 'want' it with utmost clarity. Each one of us is very dear to the Creator and He does everything required to make our wishes come true. All we have to do is 'wish' it and we get it, because He is there working for us. The entire Universe moves to our commands. Each thought, each word is a command that is carried out by the cosmic energies of the Universe. Whether the required activity takes place through us or through someone else, it will be the best that can be done to make our wishes come true. Complete trust in and surrender to the Almighty is required.

Another thing that is required is to be present in the moment. If we put our 100 per cent awareness in the present moment, we will receive everything we need. All that we require is there in the Universe and comes our way when we need it. Divine guidance comes to us when we need it. The knowledge that we need comes our way at the right time. Love, wealth, abundance, everything that we want flows freely into our lives if we allow it to. Sending out clear, positive thoughts that do not conflict with each other enables the Creator to send into our lives all that we ask for. Living in gratitude further strengthens all the positive energy that we have created in our lives.

Let us consider the example of a man who is in need of money. He goes to a temple and prays to God for wealth for about five minutes every day. The moment he steps out of the temple till the moment he steps into it again the next day, all he can think of is, "Oh God! I am so poor! I have nothing." Just imagine what God is receiving from him for twenty-three hours fifty-five minutes out of the twenty-four hours! It is obvious that poverty continues to stay in his life and he even starts believing that God doesn't listen to everyone. Conflicting and confusing messages going out from us, therefore, send confusion back into our lives. Similarly by thinking, "I am a victim of the circumstances," creates situations for us that do make us victims.

We look for happiness everywhere around us. We work hard at relationships to get happiness from them. We work hard to earn money in order to obtain happiness from it. Once in a while we take time off from our routine lives thinking that one week of holidaying is all that can give us happiness. We do all this in pursuit of happiness, while the Creator gave us the key to happiness in our own hands. If we understand our true selves, we realise that happiness is our most natural state of being. Once we acknowledge that, happiness simply overflows into every situation and every relationship around us. Then we don't have to work hard to grab happiness from a relationship, a situation, a place, etc. Whatever we do, wherever we are, happiness simply becomes our state of being.

When our child is away from us and in a tough situation, what comes to our mind instantly is the helplessness at being unable to help him because of distance or circumstances. This is because we believe we have created the child and are the almighty for him. At such times, the vibrations of helplessness, pity, worry or sympathy we generate reach our child because we are strongly connected with him. Such vibrations only weaken him. They not only drain our energies, they also disempower him. Pure love, on the other hand, empowers him and provides him strength. Another thing that can help him in a big way is our surrender to the Almighty knowing that our child is as much the Creator's child as we are. He is there with our child and *will* do whatever is required to bring him out of the situation most gracefully. This knowledge creates peace inside us while giving strength to the child. Through such power packets we actually *allow* the Creator to take care of our child. The child then naturally receives all that he requires to handle the situation in the best possible way.

Thus, a complete surrender to this omnipotent, omnipresent, all-pervading creative force is actually a way to realising our own power. It does not mean giving up. In fact, we give up our resistance to the supreme power that works only in accordance with our wishes, and in the best way, too. So, surrender is a way to self-empowerment.

Chapter 7

DON'T BE CONTROLLED

The only way to stop others from controlling me is to control them!

So often during the course of our lives, we call ourselves the victims of circumstances or even of the people around us. We feel it is the situations that control us. We carry this huge fear of being controlled by others. As a result, we start controlling others because we feel if we don't do so, they will control us which we certainly don't want.

If we feel we are being controlled by others, it is certain that the problem is again inside us. We fear that we will be controlled. Those are the vibrations others are receiving from us. We actually invite what we fear because that is what we are sending our power packets towards.

The fear that others want to control us conveys the lack of self-confidence. Others can affect us only if and when we allow them to. Self-confidence comes from accepting and loving ourselves unconditionally. Besides, if we truly surrender ourselves to the Creator, we cannot fear anyone's control over our lives. Once we eliminate from ourselves this fear of being controlled, we stop trying to control others. Accepting others as they are also enables us to allow them to lead their lives as they choose to. What we receive from them in turn is similar respect and acceptance.

We can make our journeys more interesting by sharing our joys with each other. We need each other's love and support while being on our own respective paths. Thus it is in our mutual interest to have a respectful relationship with each other.

Each one of us governs one's own life alone.

It is important to understand that it is not others that we have to change. We feel others are giving us a problem, so the problem is with them and hence *they* need to be changed. The truth is that if *we* are troubled, the source of the problem is within us. The only way we can change anything in our lives is by bringing about a change in our own selves. If we alter our attitude and our way of thinking, the Universe would start receiving positive messages from us and acting on those, it would provide us with positive situations.

Chapter 8

MATERIAL IS WELCOME

It is a tough job maintaining balance
between materialism and spiritualism, isn't it?

Well actually it isn't because both have no connection with each other.

Material is often seen as something inferior to spiritual. The former supposedly takes us away from God while the latter is believed to do the opposite, i.e. take us closer to God. This belief has developed over centuries and has formed deep roots inside us. Consequently, if we are inclined towards spiritualism to any extent, we carry beliefs against materialism. If, on the other hand, our thoughts are focussed on all that is material in this world, we believe spiritualism belongs to another world and is meant for a different genre of people.

The problem, here too, is because of some distorted beliefs and not due to materialism or spiritualism. **We can attract both in our lives at the same time, if we wish to.**

Spirituality truly is turning inwards. Our life begins from

inside us. Everything outside and around us is attracted towards us by whatever is inside us. By getting closer to our true selves, we naturally get closer to the Creator. It is through understanding our own selves better that we can experience the universal creative energy closely.

Spiritualism takes us closer to our true selves. As we do this, we get more aware of our beliefs and the power packets we send. While on this path we can receive guidance from outside but to realise the Creator of the Universe, it is necessary to realise oneself.

If we believe that spiritualism and materialism are mutually exclusive, we will be able to enjoy only one of the two: that which we are more inclined towards. The fact is that no one can stop us from experiencing both simultaneously, none other than we ourselves. If we believe materialism keeps us away from our true selves, it will. On the other hand, if we maintain the right perspective towards wealth and self-realisation, we will be able to invite both in our lives.

We have to understand that it is not a sin to long for the comforts of the physical world. People who became insensitive or less humane on acquiring material abundance are on their respective journeys and are making their own choices in their lives. We can choose to take our own individual paths. **Wealth cannot shape our lives, our power packets do.**

Wealth is looked upon as a means to improve the quality of our, and even others' lives. We can choose to be either generous or selfish with the wealth that we have. These options are always available with us, irrespective of the amount of money or wealth we possess. However, we have many more choices available to us when we have more wealth at our disposal. It does give us a certain power in the physical world. The concept of contentment begins to blur and greed tends to take its place. It becomes increasingly important to watch our karma with the increase in wealth because then the options available to us are more and it is easy to give in to the temptation of greed. At the same time, believing that since wealth leads to greed, it is better to keep it at bay only comes from a lack of belief in the self.

Let us understand the difference between greed and deserving more. Greed keeps the object of desire at the highest level of priority and provokes an individual to indulge in any kind of act to acquire the same. On the other hand, when we *know* that we deserve more of something, we also know that it is coming our way for sure. The restlessness or anxiety to grab it from anywhere, anyhow is not present. The former leads to inner turbulence whereas the latter naturally brings to us whatever we desire while we are at peace within.

Complete acceptance of and confidence in ourselves makes us realise that we deserve what we want and that it is not because we have to prove ourselves to anyone that we want wealth. At times we want more because not having it gives us a complex as we compare ourselves with others. Here the desire for wealth arises out of negative emotions of jealousy and complex. One negative emotion attracts another and can easily make us give in to greed whereas, if we live with complete acceptance of ourselves and our life as it is, our desire for wealth is unlikely to get us off balance.

When honest people leading a moderate life observe others adopting unfair means to earn wealth and succeeding at it, they develop the belief that huge amounts of money can be earned only through unfair means. If we see someone close to us become wealthy overnight due to some windfall of wealth by way of inheritance or a few great business deals, it influences us greatly. Then if we see the same person lose most of that wealth due to careless expenditure and loss in business, we start thanking our stars for not giving us too much wealth because it goes away just as fast as it comes.

Such instances that we keep seeing around us are individual stories of different people. Each one of us is creating his own life with his karma, which is different for each one of us. We can choose to pick up beliefs from the negative experiences of others and create our lives accordingly. On the other hand, we could just observe the things around us as a spectator while being confident of ourselves and watch our power packets create a life that we desire and deserve.

We always do get what we deserve, and we deserve what we believe we do.

Many of us have come across people whose attitude towards others changed for the worse after acquiring wealth. That doesn't imply that even we will become insensitive to fellow human beings if we were to become rich. If we are confident of ourselves and aware of our power to create for ourselves whatever we wish for, we will not give in to selfishness. People become selfish with their possessions because they are not sure of themselves. They feel insecure about their future. Therefore they want to save wealth for themselves for a later date. By thus sending their power packets to a likely scarcity in the future, they are actually creating what they fear — scarcity in the future!

There are people for whom wealth and property take precedence over everything else, so much so that they even pray to and remember the Creator only to maintain and increase their material possessions. The entire focus of their existence is on all that is material. Their discontentment makes them give in to greed, jealousy and insecurity. Thus they are driven far from their own inner selves, and the Creator. Yet it is not their wealth which is driving them away from the Creator. It is their own choice. Being abundant materially, we can still be connected with our true selves by watching our karma.

In watching our karma, our actions are the easiest to watch and check. Watching our words requires some practice. It is watching and correcting our thoughts, that needs maximum effort, at least initially until it becomes a habit.

Chapter 9

DE-POISON YOURSELF: ELIMINATE ANGER

I know anger isn't good for me,
but I just can't control it.

We all know that anger isn't good for us and yet we feel helpless at its hands. The more we try to control it, the more it seems to keep taking control of us. How much ever we might, in our calmer times, think about not getting angry; the moment even a small provocation occurs, it comes up like a beast that has just been let free from a cage. Only when the beast goes back, we realise what damage it did.

It is usually the imperfections we see in others that give rise to anger in us. This, in turn, comes from the lack of acceptance of things and people as they are. The root of this lack of acceptance lies in the lack of self-acceptance. We see imperfections in ourselves and are unable to accept ourselves completely. It is the frustration inside us that gets aggravated and comes out in the form of anger at someone when our inner conflict reflects in the people or situations around us.

When things aren't going our way, at home or at work, we get angry. At times the deadlines that we are working within are unreasonable and we know it. Yet, when another person we are working with is unable to meet the same unreasonable deadlines, we pour out all our frustrations on him. If we truly believe within ourselves that we *can* meet the deadline, those are the vibrations we would be giving out to those involved in the task at hand. Thus being at peace within ourselves, we wouldn't create the conflict around us.

Sometimes not being able to meet the unreasonable deadlines creates within us anger towards our own selves, too. This anger is as unreasonable as the deadline that is the cause for it. We can only do whatever is physically possible. Wasting our energy through anger cannot help us in any way. In any case, if we had believed right from the beginning that the deadline is hard to meet, there was no way we could have met it. Going about our job peacefully will at least ensure good quality of the work done.

When we delegate someone a task, we have in mind a particular result that we expect from him. Occasionally that is not exactly what we get from that person. When we find the result completely different from what we had expected, we are unable to accept it. Instead of calmly assessing the situation as to why it happened, we simply give in to anger that flares up in us that instant. The reason could have been lack of proper communication on our part to him about what we had expected, or a mismatch between the skills of that person and those required for the job to be completed. Having understood the reason of the fiasco helps us act more wisely in the future. Accepting the situation as it is helps us keep anger at bay. Then we can consider what can be done to amend the situation in the best possible way. By getting angry we would only be giving negative vibrations not only to the task and the other person involved, but also to ourselves. This drains our energy and we are unable to think of the best way to improvise the situation.

Trust is another prerequisite for delegation. At times when we delegate a task, we are not sure whether the person we are delegating the task to is capable of doing it well. The solution is to either find the right person to do the job or to train the person appropriately for the same. Giving a person a job and doubting his capability to do it at the same time can create a situation wherein he either can't do it or is unable to do it according to our expectations. The conflict already present inside us then takes the form of anger towards that person. It is better to ensure our trust in the person we are delegating the work to, rather than harbour negative feelings about it and then wait for them to work against us.

At times we have expectations from ourselves that we know are unreasonable, simply because someone else expects them out of us. Cultivating self-confidence within ourselves brings a calm inside us that keeps us centred. When we are centred, external stimuli don't make us lose the right perspective to things around us. This helps us take the right decisions of where, when and how to express ourselves, instead of continually taking on others' expectations that they have from us even when we know they are unreasonable. When we do something for the sake of meeting someone's expectations and not because *we* want to do it, it results in anger and frustration.

Sometimes it is what someone says to us that incites anger in us. We feel insulted by that person and that, for us, is reason enough to get angry at him. By getting angry, though, we only harm ourselves. So it is *our* choice to give the power to that person and his words to be able to harm us. If that person's words have hurt us, we have an opportunity to look into ourselves to find out what inside us got triggered by that person's words. If we know ourselves well and love and accept ourselves as we are, nothing from outside can disturb us. Then, whatever a person says to us merely reflects his view and can be used for guidance in our future dealings with him.

The need is to eliminate these causes of anger rather than trying to control anger itself. Once anger has arisen, we can't control it. It instantly creates a disorder in the mind thereby leaving no room for reason. It not only harms us by making us say and do things that we often regret later, it even makes us hate ourselves later for having behaved that way.

Anger, like any other negative emotion, stems from some inner conflicts. In the absence of any check on those conflicts, it grows as a habit in us day by day till it takes full control over us.

Stress causes anger and that, in turn, causes further stress. This vicious circle creates toxins which get accumulated in our bodies. This is how anger acts as poison. Eliminating anger from our personalities is as good as de-poisoning ourselves.

Once we acknowledge the problem we are facing, our mind shifts its focus on finding its solution. Therefore, once we realise that we have to conquer our anger, we can begin by watching it every time we experience it. When we get angry, we are unable to calm down instantly. However, by making ourselves aware at that time that we are angry makes us alert to the things we say and do, even if the situation is not much in our control. Thus we take at least some power away from the anger by regaining our awareness back to ourselves, even if to a small extent. The anger can thus be kept within bounds and then it also recedes faster.

This should be followed by a self-analysis about what triggered off anger in us at that time. What was it about the other person or the situation that made us angry? What does that reflect about our own selves, about our self-love and acceptance, about the expectations we carry of ourselves and of others, etc.

Watching our anger every time it comes and later analysing its cause, followed by working to eliminate that cause decreases the frequency of occurrence of anger in our lives and greatly helps in slowly eliminating it altogether. Judging ourselves on our behaviour during the time we were angry will only have us sucked up into a vortex of negative feelings for ourselves. Eliminating the cause of anger in us and hence the anger itself is what we need to focus on.

At times anger is useful. We have discussed earlier that passive acceptance of whatever negative is there around us does not lead to much improvement in our lives. When we experience any situation around us that is undesirable; injustice, for example, we do get angry. That anger, if within our awareness, gives us energy that we can harness to bring about a change in that undesirable situation. Rather than giving in our power to the anger, we can use the force of anger to take the required action. Once the action has been taken though, the anger must be dropped.

It is self-knowledge, therefore, that helps us in getting rid of all that is undesirable in us. We can begin living in awareness of ourselves by watching our thoughts.

There is no need to judge ourselves on the basis of the thoughts that emerge. Only, the patterns we realise as negative need to be shed and replaced with the corresponding positive ones.

SECTION III

EMPOWER YOUR RELATIONSHIPS

Chapter 10

RELATIONSHIPS

Why do they drain us so much?

We are surrounded with relationships all the time: at home, school, work, everywhere. Relationships can be a source of happiness for us, but at times they give us stress. Sometimes they boost our energies while at times they drain them.

At home, relationships are most important. At the end of the day, everyone looks for the relaxation the comforts of a home and the warmth of a loving family provide. At school, the child not only grows in knowledge but also learns some important skills in communication and interaction through his dealings with the classmates and teachers. If the child shares a good rapport with the teachers and has good friends at school, the school journey becomes very enjoyable and memorable. In fact, some of the friends made at school are lifelong support systems for most of the people.

Relationships are very important at work, too. Almost every kind of work involves at least some interaction with others.

The kind of relationship one has with one's boss and the subordinates decides the growth of the person in his job to a certain extent. It is not flattery that always works with a boss. The individual's capability of providing good output in work is a basic requirement, but is not all that can bring about career growth for him. Sharing a healthy relationship with the boss as well as the subordinates usually enables a person to do even better at work and progress faster. Also how one interacts with one's peers decides the amount of stress one develops at work.

Relationships in life make it more enjoyable for us. They are there for us to experience the most beautiful form of energy — love. **Love truly is the essence of life.** Yet what we experience in different relationships is not only love and happiness. One avoidable, yet inevitable, part of any relationship is expectations. As two people get closer in any relationship, each one starts developing expectations from the other. Then each person involved starts looking at the other with respect to his own expectations of the other. This leads to passing judgements. This is different from accepting the other person completely, just as he is.

Expectations between two people kill the spontaneity in their relationship, and lead to negative emotions like blame and guilt.

For a relationship to be ideal, i.e. full of pure love for each other, the first and the foremost need is to accept the other person as he is, unconditionally. We might not agree with the other person's views or ways. We can voice our opinion/advice, but the other person certainly has the right to live according to his beliefs, views and ways just as we have to ours. At the same time, not meeting the other's expectations shouldn't give us any guilt, either. In any relationship, each one ought to be oneself, simply truly oneself.

Relationships give meaning to our lives. They give us a reason to go on. So, any relationship that brings our morale down, isn't worth being there in our lives. At times if a friendship has gone sour, we have to drop a name from the list of our friends, or we have to distance ourselves from a certain relative. This is not always possible, though. When we realise we have to, for certain reasons, accept such a relationship in our lives; we must give it love, and lots of it.

Pure unconditional love is a powerful positive energy that can slowly dissolve all negative energies like those of blame, guilt and revenge.

Blame can lead to guilt or revenge; and revenge by one can lead to the same reaction from the other. Negative energies thus keep on accumulating. So, they don't really serve any purpose other than to destroy and damage a relationship. Whatever unpleasant might have happened in a relationship in the past shouldn't be allowed to guide our feelings for the other person in the future. As we begin giving a relationship our pure unconditional love and stop focussing what gave us unhappiness in the past, we can develop a new bonding with that person — full of love and respect for each other.

In any relationship, both the persons involved need to appreciate the fact that they are in their own respective long journeys; together just for a while. Doing things that make this togetherness enjoyable for both enriches their lives.

In a relationship, even when everything is going fine, a problem can begin anytime if we don't like what the other person says or does to us. We might feel the other person took us for granted, insulted us in some way or misunderstood us in certain respect. It is very interesting to note that anyone can take us for granted only if somewhere inside us we believe that we deserve to be taken for granted. For example, in the process of bringing up her child, in the initial few years a mother usually unknowingly allows the child to take her for granted, in order to be always available for any help the child might need anytime. So much so, that if due to some preoccupation she has to delay her child's meal even by a few minutes, she feels guilty because she feels solely responsible to meet all the needs of the child. These are the vibrations the child receives from his mother while he is growing up even though the mother is not quite conscious of it. Later on, when the child grows up and throws tantrums she feels miserable that the child takes her for granted. So we must look into ourselves for the erroneous vibrations we might be sending out that allowed someone to take us for granted.

Similarly, if we feel insulted by someone, we must check if we respect ourselves truly and completely. It may sound absurd that we do not respect ourselves completely. Yet if we feel there have been incidents in our lives when we felt deeply humiliated, there certainly is a belief in us that we deserve humiliation. It could be stemming from some hidden guilt we have been carrying for long or lack of self-confidence. Introspection and watching our thoughts can lead us to the cause and we have to eliminate it by giving energy to the corresponding positive belief.

If people around us misunderstand us, we must look inside and ask whether we understand ourselves completely. We feel helpless when others misunderstand us, but the key to our empowerment is inside us. There definitely is some confusion we need to sort out in our own mind. The earlier we recognise our internal confusion, the sooner we can resolve it and stop sending our power packets in wrong directions in the Universe. Whether it is a confusion about what we desire the most i.e. confusion about our priorities or about whether or not to express ourselves for fear of hurting someone which we don't want to;

there definitely is something in us that we ourselves need clarity about. Until and unless we identify and resolve it, we are bound to be faced with similar situations repeatedly.

When we are clear and confident about ourselves, what comes from outside and around us doesn't perturb us. If and when anything does, all we need to do is look inside to search what it was in us that invited it. When we live with self-knowledge, we live in peace and harmony. Then we don't live at the mercy of others' opinions. We know how to give unconditional love to everyone around us, irrespective of what they say or do to us. That is when we start living in eternal peace and harmony. Focussing on any negative vibrations coming our way will only energise them and increase sadness in our lives. We can dispel them by sending unconditional love to their source.

Be conscious of what you are giving to the relationships built around you because whatever you give comes back to you multifold.

Chapter 11

UNCONDITIONAL LOVE

Love everyone unconditionally — how is that possible?

This is a question that comes to our mind when we hear about having unconditional love for everyone. To be honest, I used to ask this question myself till a few years back; not anymore.

We truly are unconditional love. It is only because we spend our lifetimes fighting our own selves that we forget our true nature. Our thoughts are always scattered in various directions: towards people, situations, various judgements we are busy passing, various expectations we are harbouring inside, the comparisons we keep making of ourselves with others, the complexes inside us, and so on. We never have the time or the inclination to understand our true selves. So, our power packets have been going waste. In fact, they have been used to create conflicts for us. So many of them have been sent to negative energies like jealousy, blame, etc. when we only crave to experience love, peace and happiness. Once we decide to get closer to our true nature, we start eliminating all negative thoughts that we are so used to generating. This takes some time, but more than that it requires the intention and determination to do so. As we start creating more and more positive beliefs within ourselves, they generate only positive thoughts within us.

Slowly, we realise that there is only one extremely powerful energy that creates happiness within and around us: the unconditional love that we are!

At times we even judge the Creator on the basis of what we experience in life, holding Him responsible for all the miseries that we suffer. With better knowledge about our lives, we learn to send our unconditional love the Creator's way, and that is exactly what we experience coming our way from Him. As we have seen earlier, we tend to keep blaming ourselves for the various faults we perceive in us. As a result we fail to love and accept ourselves unconditionally. If we want to truly love and respect our Creator, we have to love and accept ourselves unconditionally, because that is what *He* does. Once we are full of love for the Creator and ourselves, it doesn't require much effort in extending the same to everyone around us. Once we realise that everyone is what we are and that He made everyone with His own energy, we begin seeing everyone as a part of Him. In a way we all are the same: His reflections. He loves each one of us without any discrimination. Realising this makes it easy and natural to love everyone unconditionally. It stems from within, from a feeling of completeness within us.

Going by this theory, self-knowledge and self-love is a prerequisite to experiencing unconditional love for all. There is another way of doing it too. If we can simply start practising loving ourselves unconditionally, all the negativities we carry will dissolve in it by and by, and before long unconditional love will become our way of living. It depends upon the individual, which way he chooses to do it.

Love is to life what blood is to body.

Just as the strength in the body is proportionate to the amount of blood in it, the zeal for life in an individual is directly proportional to how much unconditional love he experiences. There is immense love inside us. Love and happiness describe our natural state of being. That is the reason when we are in love we experience a never ending source of energy inside us, whereas emotions like hatred and anger always drain our energies, resulting in stress.

Love is not something that is given or taken. It is something that is just experienced.

As we feel love inside, its vibrations flow out naturally and reach those around us. As it flows out from us to the others, we never feel the lack of it. In fact it comes back multifold. It is such a powerful positive energy that if we think of our loved ones with unconditional love, it dissolves the negativity inside and around them. Hence, the more power packets we give to this energy, the better for us and those dear to us.

When we start living with a complete acceptance and with a sense of surrender to Creator, we begin the process of releasing all that is negative from within and empower ourselves. Realising the unconditional love that we are full of further empowers us. Let us then give this unconditional love to not only ourselves and others, but also to each and every activity that we are involved in.

Young mothers have often noticed that they rarely fall ill as long as their child is an infant. That is because the mother of an infant knows her child is completely dependent on her for everything. So if she falls ill even for a day, the child's life that day will become totally chaotic which she can't bear to see. So she 'knows' it for sure that she has to be healthy. This is a very powerful example that conveys two important things. One, when we 'know' something from inside, it is different from having to tell ourselves the same thing. When we 'know' it, we acknowledge it as a fact. There is no other way to it. So we don't send any power packets to doubt it. On the other hand, when we tell ourselves something, e.g. 'my leg pain will go away', the next day we also wonder and check whether it did go away. Obviously, we were not sure whether the pain will go. We were trying to inculcate the positive belief in ourselves, at the same time checking to see whether it works. It will work for us much better if we 'know' that it will work for sure, and stop doubting it. Unconditional love brings energy when we put it wholeheartedly into whatever we do. The newly arrived baby is very precious to the mother. She has only love for him and happily devotes all twenty-four hours of the day looking after him. As a result, even the twenty-four hour duty doesn't tire her. If we could bring that kind of love into whatever we are involved in every moment, nothing can drain our energies. It doesn't require much. Being present in the moment with our full awareness is what it takes.

Let's consider a homemaker who dislikes the activity of cooking meals for her family everyday because she finds it too monotonous. When she cooks every day, she often thinks of other interesting activities she could be doing during that time instead. Doing that, though, doesn't help her in any way because it is still the cooking that she has to do during that time and not the other activities she is thinking of. If she puts her presence and love in the cooking that she is engaged in, she will not only be able to produce tastier meals, the time spent in making it will also give her relaxation rather than frustration.

If you have to do something that you don't like to, it is better not to do it than to do it grudgingly. The latter will not only ruin your internal peace but the job being done, as well. If you must do it, then do it with acceptance and love. This naturally and effortlessly improves the quality of the work done besides creating positive vibrations inside.

Chapter 12

PERFECTION IS A MIRAGE

Isn't perfection always the best way to be,
for everyone and everything?

Most of us aspire to be perfect in whatever we do. This is a good attitude, but not if we find ourselves completely acceptable only when we are perfect.

Can you define *perfection*? Supposing you do, are you sure it is a 'perfect' definition and will never change with time for you?

Usually, with time, as we acquire the quality that we had thought would make us perfect, we find something else lacking in ourselves.

Why then, are we aiming for perfection all the time and punishing ourselves by rejecting ourselves our complete and unconditional acceptance for not reaching there — the point of perfection? The fact is that even when we do reach there our definition of perfection goes a notch higher!

We keep comparing ourselves with others that we meet and know. All those qualities that we like in others and aspire to have in ourselves put together with all those that we like in ourselves, kind of defines *perfection* for us. We aspire to be the perfect one with all those qualities, each to a level ten on a scale of one to ten.

Again we need to remember that each one of us is at a different stage in our own individual journey. Each one of us has been through different experiences, learnt different lessons and has specific needs. Our experiences are based on the lessons we need to learn in order to grow and evolve. Therefore, each one of us is here on the planet at any particular time to learn different lessons. Our personalities are governed by all that we have learnt and all that we are learning. It can never be exactly the same for any two of us at any given time. We need to respect ourselves for what we are and accept ourselves wholeheartedly.

Truly, we are perfect as we are.

This is the only way we could and would have been. If we love and accept ourselves completely, it becomes effortless to move on to the next stage of our evolution where we can be as we now aspire to be.

In order to accept ourselves fully, we need to own the choices we have made during our journey to be where we are now. We are constantly evolving. We had aspired to be where and what we are, hence we are. If we accept that, we can smoothly become what we now aspire to be.

Remember, our Creator always finds us perfect just as we are. That's why He is carrying out our instructions (that He receives through our thoughts, speech and actions) with the same love and consistency always. The concept of perfection probably doesn't even exist for the Creator because nothing for Him is anything less or more than perfect!

Chapter 13

EXPECTATIONS OR LIBERATION

Isn't it very natural to have expectations from those we share our lives with?

These expectations cause most relationships to go through turbulences.

Expectations covertly creep into our minds and play an important role in creating happiness or unhappiness. Interestingly, that is the amount of power we give them.

When we expect, we also doubt. If we 'want' something and we *know* we deserve it, we would also know that it is going to come our way for sure. This is against 'expecting' it where we 'hope' to get it and not getting it would make us unhappy.

When we expect from others, it indicates that we are not sure of ourselves.

When a mother-in-law expects her daughter-in-law to respect her in a certain manner, she isn't sure she deserves that respect, or it would come to her naturally. When a parent expects her son to stand first in his class, she isn't sure her son will do well in his studies and also in his life, irrespective of what position he scores. When a wife expects her husband to load her with expensive gifts every now and then, she isn't sure she deserves to be and is truly loved by him and all that she desires will anyway come her way through him or any other way if she truly believes she deserves it. Thus, instead of giving our power packets to the object of our desire and our worthiness for it, we are wasting them on deciding the source from where it should come to us and also on the doubt whether or not it will come to us. Expectations, therefore, are doing more harm to us than good.

Expectations also arise from lack of acceptance.

Parents who have been unable to achieve their goals in their young age aspire to see their children achieve those very goals in their lives. They couldn't accept that whatever they did get was what they actually did create for themselves, no matter what it was that they were consciously trying to achieve. They also are unable to understand that their child is on his own journey and has a path of his own to follow. They find it difficult to accept that he could bloom and prosper better on any path different from what they chose for him. If what they choose for him is not in sync with the path his soul aspires to follow, it could lead to lifelong misery for both, the child and the parents.

Each one of us is here to follow our own specific paths, while sharing our lives with each other. We all do serve some purpose in the lives of those around us and close to us. Sometimes though, we get driven by what we think is expected out of us by others. At times such expectations that others have from us are directly conveyed by them. Sometimes we, rightly or wrongly, presume them. It makes us happy to do only the things that we truly want to and would love to do for others.

Forcing ourselves to do something for the sake of others simply because they expect it from us creates blame energy inside us. Doing things that give us happiness will naturally create happiness for others, too. If there is something that we must do even if we don't like doing it, there must be a good reason *why* we must do it. If that reason is important enough for us, we need to create a complete understanding and unconditional love and acceptance for that reason in ourselves. Then we would be doing that activity out of our own will and not to meet any expectation.

We even expect a lot from ourselves all the time. We do so because we are running after the imaginary concept of perfection. We have goals to achieve in our personal and professional lives. We are constantly working towards these goals. If we do so with complete confidence in ourselves as well as belief in the goals we are aiming at, we do achieve them. If the results we achieve are different from what we expected, we find it difficult to accept them and start judging ourselves for having been right or wrong at different points in our efforts. If we could just accept the results we have created, learn from the experience and use that learning to continue working towards our goals, we could eliminate stress from our lives that our expectations create for us.

The basic and the most powerful form of positive energy: unconditional love and acceptance for ourselves annihilates any need for expectation. **Expectations weigh us down while love liberates!**

Chapter 14

PENDULUM OF BLAME AND GUILT

We blame someone only when they hurt us...

We blame others when we feel unhappy due to something that someone did. We again forget that everything in our lives has been created by our own selves. We have expectations from others. When others don't act according to our expectations, it makes us unhappy and we blame them for our unhappiness.

India at present is deeply influenced by the Western culture. Yet the roots of our own traditions are deeply engraved in us. Here girls grow up with the knowledge that one day it is another family that they have to adopt as their own and nurture. Hence they try their best to make everyone in their new family happy and in the process get miserable themselves. This is not because of anything wrong in our culture but due to some distorted beliefs. Girls see and hear their mothers and aunts complain about the sacrifices and sufferings they went through for their in-laws and grow up with the belief that this is a norm. In trying to fight this belief, they struggle hard to prove themselves as the ideal daughters-in-law. What is missing here, though, is self-acceptance and self-love. We tend to forget that we cannot give happiness to anyone until we ourselves are happy inside.

We sacrifice ourselves only when we don't love ourselves enough. Sacrifice, therefore, doesn't involve positive energy. Anything that doesn't come from positive energy cannot create peace and harmony. If a daughter-in-law finds things in her new family that are completely against her expectations, she has only two options: either leave the family forever or accept it completely. If she leaves, she will still be living with the beliefs that created for her the situations that gave her the trauma. By owning up the complete responsibility of our lives and accepting wholeheartedly what we have created for ourselves, we can start improving the quality of our lives.

Four brothers grew up together in one house and started assisting their father in his business. Soon they had their individual units of business to look after. One of them started prospering much faster than the others and soon became one of the richest men in the city. While enjoying his success, he was also concerned about his brothers. He would help them as and when he could, but the problem was the secret guilt he had developed inside, of enjoying prosperity alone while his brothers couldn't. Unaware, he was sending these vibes to his brothers, thus inviting trouble for himself. The brothers started taking him for granted, never acknowledging the help and support they always received from him and kept asking for more than before. The rich brother was in anguish. It was not wrong on his part to help his brothers. If he had kept guilt out of the picture, though, he could have moved on with his life happily while feeling content with whatever support he could provide them. Even born and brought up as siblings, any two brothers or sisters are two individual souls on their own journeys. They are together because there are certain things they want to share during that common phase of their journeys. Each one still has to live one's own karma. Guilt on the part of the rich brother and blaming on the part of the other brothers was all futile and a waste of their precious energies.

To think that it is the situations that we are in and the people we have to interact with that make us miserable is running away from our own selves and can then lead to lifelong misery. No one can affect us until we allow them to. During our past experiences we have learnt certain lessons and developed certain beliefs in order to avoid certain kind of misery, little realising that the new beliefs might lead us to another kind of despair. A businessman who worked hard to take his business to the heights of success, during his old age, saw his son ruin his entire business by and by. He was agonised to see his lifetime of efforts go down the drain and would often say to himself that he would have been better off without a son. In the next lifetime he became a businessman again and never had a son. That was the result of his own prayers having been answered. Unaware of this fact, he ignorantly would often blame God for not having blessed him with a son who would have handled his business in his old age.

Thus, **it is in our ignorance that we blame**. Blaming never helps us. It is a negative energy that we allow to develop inside us. Negative energies like blame and anger, if unchecked, have a tendency to shroud our reasoning power. They lead us to revenge, which is another very strong negative emotion. These negative emotions sometimes make us do things that our conscience doesn't agree with, thus creating conflicts inside us, later leading to guilt. This is how, if we allow these negative emotions to prosper, we keep drifting from one to the other like a pendulum that never stops.

Whenever we do something, we do what we think is right. The same is true for others. At any point in time, even they do only what they think is right for them. At that time, if our 'right' doesn't match with theirs, for whatever reason, we blame them. If at a later point in time our 'right' doesn't match with our own 'right' at the time when we did something, we develop guilt for having done something 'wrong'. Isn't all this pointless? Whatever has been done, *has* been done. What can be achieved through blame and guilt, other than creating negative energy in ourselves and our lives? There is nothing better than accepting whatever has happened as a part of living our own karma. Watching our karma from the current moment onwards is what can help dispel all negativity from our lives.

Chapter 15

REVENGE OR HAPPINESS

If someone has hurt me deeply, he must pay for it.

This thought comes very naturally to us when someone we have been dealing with hurts or cheats us. We want to see that person suffer as we have suffered because of him.

The truth is that we never suffer because of anyone else. We suffer because of our own karma. Our karma is our response to the people and situations around us. It is with us in our journey in the form of subconscious beliefs. Even though the subconscious is inaccessible, it does present itself in the form of our thoughts. If we learn to watch and be conscious of our innermost thoughts, we can identify the thought patterns arising out of the negative beliefs held in our subconscious. These are the ones that create negative situations for us. People around us simply act as a medium for conveying those miseries to us. We get only what we attract through our thoughts.

Hence if someone cheated us, it will help us to identify trust related beliefs within us. We might consciously have tried to trust someone, but at a deeper level, do we really believe in trusting others or do we feel it is unsafe to trust others? Do we know how to trust someone? If someone has insulted us, we need to look within to determine if we respect ourselves completely and believe that we *deserve* the respect we are consciously looking for. Lack of self-love is common, and leads to lack of self-respect, naturally inviting humiliation from outside.

Every situation in our lives that makes us unhappy or uncomfortable in any way is an opportunity to look within and release some negative beliefs held by us.

If someone has let us down, we need to ask ourselves whether *we* respected that person. It is one of the laws of the Universe that what goes from us is what comes back to us. If we find it difficult to respect someone, it would be even harder to earn respect for ourselves from him.

Strongly feeling the need to avenge someone for having hurt us not only keeps reminding us of the hurt we suffered, hence making us relive the experience over and over again for long after it has become history, it also nurtures within us negative emotions of anger and hatred. All these take us away from our true nature of love, peace and happiness. Something that takes our peace and happiness away from us is not worth keeping, even if it means pardoning someone who, apparently, has harmed us.

This, by no means, is the same as giving signals to that person that it is alright for him to harm us again. Those were the signals he actually received from us in the first place, to have been able to affect us negatively. We need to find out by introspection the cause inside us of having given those signals, and eliminate it from within. Once we are thus confident of ourselves, no one can adversely affect us in any way.

If someone has harmed us, it was only because we gave them the power to do so.

Often we get to hear, "I gave him so much love, affection and respect and look how he has cheated on me!" If we truly, completely and unconditionally love and accept our own selves, we don't *have to* love and respect anyone else. It is then just our natural way of being. Then we don't have to keep an account of how much we did for someone because it ceases to be an effort. We remember doing something only when it is an effort on our part. We have to make efforts to do something only when doing that does not come naturally to us. Doing something for someone purely out of duty or out of some expectation in return is an effort and does not stem from love.

Therefore, if we live in complete love and acceptance of ourselves, there is no room for negative emotions like hatred and revenge. Love attracts all that is positive into our lives and enables us to lead a happy life. Revenge, before harming the one we want to avenge, harms us deeply in multiple ways. Why, then, choose revenge over happiness?

Chapter 16

JUDGEMENT

Isn't it necessary to notice and point out if anyone around us is doing wrong?

We have seen that unconditional acceptance of people (including ourselves) and things as they are is a prerequisite for being able to live in peace and realise our power. Constantly judging ourselves and others is a huge block in way of unconditional acceptance.

Judgements crop up from our beliefs of right and wrong. There can't be an absolute definition of *right*. What seems right to us might appear wrong to others. What seems right to us now might appear wrong to us sometime later, after we have gained some more experience. The fact is that anyone does, at any point of time, what he thinks is right. No one does anything thinking it is wrong to do it. Our opinions can differ but that doesn't take away the right of others or ours to do what they/we want to do. If we don't like what others are doing and it affects us in some way, we can use our discernment by either telling them that we disagree with them and take decisions about further dealings with them based on their reaction, or simply dissociate ourselves from them.

What we think is the truth, is how it *appears* to us. The same thing might seem different to others, according to their perspective. That is *their* truth. Neither is wrong. When we in India think it is day, those in the US think it is night. It is only after complete knowledge about the earth and the solar system was discovered and made known to us that we could understand how it could be night for others when it is day for us. Similarly, with experience and knowledge we learn to understand the others' perspective. Therefore, there is no absolute *right* or *wrong*. Whatever others do in their own lives is their right. It is futile passing judgements about someone being right or wrong.

It is lack of self-acceptance that makes us judge ourselves. When we realise we have been wrong somewhere, it can lead to guilt or even self-hatred. Allowing these negative energies to grow within takes away peace and happiness from us. The learning we obtain from our experiences should be used to take the necessary action to improvise the situation and not to pass judgements about ourselves and our actions.

Judging others also actually comes from lack of complete self-acceptance. We tend to keep comparing ourselves with others. If we find ourselves less than or worse than others, it gives rise to an inferiority complex within. We further keep comparing ourselves with others to see where we are better than them. To cover up the inferiority in ourselves, we fuel a superiority complex inside us.

Inferiority or superiority, any complex in us only complicates our lives. If we just enjoy being what we are naturally and be full of unconditional love for ourselves, there is no room for or need for judging anyone. The Creator never judges us, then why should we?

Chapter 17

JEALOUSY OR ABUNDANCE

When I see someone with something that I deserve even more (or at least as much) and yet don't have it, isn't it natural for me to feel jealous?

When we feel jealous of someone, we forget that each one of us is in our own individual journey and we have created our own lives for ourselves. Each one of us is living one's own karma.

When we compare ourselves with others, we look at one aspect of our lives or personalities, or at most a few. If we take a person as a whole, no two persons can ever be compared with each other. All of us are souls at different stages in our respective journeys. We have worked through our beliefs, thoughts, words and actions to be exactly where we are today, and none other than we ourselves are responsible for it.

What appears as truth is usually a part of the complete truth. Based on a small part of someone else's life's truth, if we harbour negative emotions like jealousy in us, we harm ourselves in more ways than one. We are then not only ruining our own peace of mind but also focussing on something that we don't have, thus giving energy to the scarcity instead of giving it to the abundance in our lives. Thus we are wasting away our power by sending our power packets in a direction that will create only misery for us.

It is our confidence in ourselves and having a clear picture in mind, of what we want, that brings us the desired results; not our comparison with others.

Consider four team leaders A, B, C and D working for a company under one manager. Each one of them is competing to impress the boss in order to get further in their careers faster. One day, B comes up with an idea that the boss is very impressed with. He then directs all four team leaders to implement the new idea with the help of their respective teams. A, C and D are so jealous of B at this point that even before listening to the complete implementation plan, they have made up their minds that they are not going to allow the implementation to be successful. So, while pretending to implement the idea as planned, they are continuously sending their power packets to its failure. Needless to say, the implementation never reaches its completion. The peers of B had intended B's idea to fail so that he doesn't score any brownie points with the boss. Was it only B who failed, though? Didn't all of them waste their time and energies doing something they never wanted to? Not doing it was not an option they had. Making it fail didn't help them either. If B failed, they didn't succeed either. It is our lives we affect. They couldn't stop B's growth if B didn't allow them to. By wasting their time and energies, though, they could delay their own career growth.

Trying to harm someone in any way can never allow us to love and accept ourselves completely, which is a basic requirement for self-confidence. It is by building up confidence in ourselves that we can get closer to our goals easily.

Jealousy often comes from a fear of being left behind others, as if all of us were together in a race. We often tend to compare our material success with those close to us: either close relatives, friends or even neighbours. Creating positive or negative feelings in our hearts for those around us is our choice, too, and each choice that we make directly affects our lives.

If we look at our lives objectively, each one of us will find a lot to be grateful to the Creator for. That is the abundance in our lives. It could be in the area of wealth, property, relationships, love and support of friends, the comfort of a home, a loving family, health, or anything else. Besides, the Universe is full of abundance of all sorts that we can further invite into our lives by sending our power packets in the right direction. Through jealousy we only focus on what we don't have, thus energising the lack in our lives. So, if at some point in life we find it 'just natural' to feel jealous of someone, we need to remind ourselves that **jealousy cannot lead us to the abundance we are looking for.**

Chapter 18

INSECURITY

The uncertainties in life often lead to insecurity within us.

How we wish to know our future! Since the future is obscure, it leads to uncertainty in our minds and that, in turn, leads to insecurity within us. When we are insecure, we are miserable and this misery overflows from us to those around us.

If we are wealthy, we are unsure if the wealth will continue to stay with us in future. If we are unhealthy, we are afraid of our health deteriorating further. Students are insecure about their results and admissions. Employees are insecure about their promotions and career growth. Businessmen are insecure about the future growth of their business. Those who are ageing are insecure about their remaining healthy and being looked after in their old age. Insecurity can creep into our thought systems at any stage in our lives, but only if we allow it to.

What really does lead to our being insecure? Lack of confidence in ourselves and lack of trust in the Creator truly does. Our belief in ourselves makes it easier for us to realise our power to create our kind of lives for ourselves. We simply need to be clear about what we really want. Trust in and surrender to the Creator effortlessly delivers us what we yearn for. If we make an effort at watching our thought packets, we can identify those that are going against our self-confidence and trust in the Creator. We need to correct those.

When we are confident of ourselves, we give our thought packets to our goals and to our power to realise them, instead of wasting them away at others who we fear can affect our future adversely. The wealthy need to understand their power with which they have created their wealth and can continue doing so and maintaining it rather than believing that others can take it away from them. Ageing parents would do well to have faith in the Creator to always take care of them through themselves, their children or anybody else, and to give them the kind of life they wish to lead in their old age. Sending their power packets to distrust in their children will only create misery inside and around them. Students, if they believe in themselves and focus on their goals, can achieve them irrespective of how their fellow students are faring. Similarly, complete confidence and belief in the self and in the Creator will keep all the employees and businessmen happily on their growth path, irrespective of the growth patterns of their peers and rivals.

In the process of bringing up their children, specially in countries like India the parents usually look upon their sons as the ones who will look after them in their old age. In most cases, the sons also grow up with the knowledge of this expectation their parents have from them. Problems, however, begin soon after the son gets married and his wife comes into the picture. The son has entered a new phase of his life and expects a lot of joy from it. The same is true for his wife. They are in the process of getting to know each other and accepting each other into their lives completely. For two individuals born and brought up in two different environments, this demands effort and time. Naturally, they tend to focus a lot on this new relationship and each other soon after the marriage. At the same time, the in-laws have a lot of expectations from the newly arrived daughter-in-law. The mother-in-law looks at each and every action and reaction of the newly wedded girl from the filters of her own expectations. Here begins a series of reactions on her part which take the daughter-in-law by surprise as she was quite unaware of the specific expectations her mother-in-law had from her.

So even though disturbances in the family might show up much later, the seeds are actually sown right in the beginning of the marriage. The daughter-in-law, who was trying to find her bearings amidst a new family and environment through her husband responds to the in-laws' reactions by developing a sense of insecurity.

We are insecure only when we try to take the reigns of our lives in our own hands. We do so when we lack trust in the Creator. If we entrust our lives completely into the Creator's hands, only what is the best for us would come our way. If we have this trust for Him within us, there really is no room for insecurity. It is the lack of trust in ourselves and the Creator that takes the form of lack of trust in our dear ones, be it our son, daughter-in-law or mother-in-law.

Insecurity can never bring to us what we are insecure about. It only brings us misery. To get rid of it, we need to change our attitude drastically. Once we acknowledge the need to do so and start becoming aware of our power packets going the wrong way, we can correct them and lead a happier life where any kind of insecurity doesn't figure.

SECTION IV

EMPOWER YOUR PHYSICAL BODY

Chapter 19

THE PHYSICAL BODY

Is my body more than the physical body I can see?

Just like everything else in the Universe, our being is also a form of energy. Our complete body is much more than what is visible to the normal human eye. The part that is, is known as the physical body. It is a small part of our complete body. Each thought arising within us is also an energy form of a particular vibration and affects a particular organ of our physical body. That's how our physical health, to a large extent, represents the various beliefs and thoughts we carry.

This is another very empowering fact because this means that the various problems we suffer through our physical body actually have their root within us. This further implies that it is within our domain to heal our physical body by correcting our beliefs and thoughts.

Each organ in our physical body is meant for carrying out one or more specific functions in our routine life. It is the thoughts concerning those related functions or aspects in our lives that affect that particular organ of our body. For example, the throat is our centre for communication. Therefore, one who faces problems in self-expression, is hesitant about the same or is usually unable to express himself clearly will be faced with throat related diseases often. Most of us have experienced at some time or the other that when we spoke the truth forthrightly, it was not received well. If that experience had too deep an impact on us, it could have led us to develop a belief that it is unsafe for us to speak the truth. This belief, too, would certainly adversely affect our throat.

Positioned near the throat is the thyroid gland, which controls the functioning of various other hormonal glands in our body. It is these hormonal glands that ensure the smooth functioning of our body. Adrenal glands also control the functioning of other hormonal glands. People with whom control is an issue in life: they fear being controlled by others thereby tending to control others themselves, develop the problems of hyperactive or under active thyroid /adrenal glands.

Those of us who live our lives believing we have too many responsibilities on our shoulders, often suffer from cervical spondilitis. The problem really doesn't lie with the responsibilities but with our attitude towards them. Our awareness of our responsibilities and our surrender to the Almighty is enough to have all of them fulfilled without straining us. All the resources we need to carry out our duties are then naturally made available to us, in the best possible way.

Even though love is the basic need of our being and is also what we are constituted of, various negative beliefs we develop over time due to some of our unpleasant experiences prohibit us from fully experiencing this bliss. This slowly leads us to heart related problems. As we near old age, we realise that time is slipping by and we haven't lived our life to the full. This happens because we have, due to various reasons, kept ourselves away from experiencing pure unconditional love which is the essence of our being. This can even lead to a heart attack.

There was a person who worked as an accounting clerk with a leading MNC. He and his family told the girl he was getting married to and her parents that he was a manager with that company. When the girl found out the truth after marriage, she was hurt at having been cheated, especially by the one she had married. She was bitter with resentment. Her husband also started feeling guilty. After that, however hard he tried to grow in his career, he failed at all his pre-promotion interviews repeatedly. The marital discord kept getting worse. One fine day we heard of him having died of a brain tumour. Everyone was dumbstruck and kept wondering, "How come all of a sudden this happened to him?" The fact was that it didn't happen all of a sudden or out of the blue. Nothing ever does. It was the guilt he had developed about his intelligence and capability to meet his wife's expectations that killed him!

A friend of mine I have mentioned about earlier in the book had been upset about having to lead the life of a homemaker instead of pursuing her career because of her husband's transfer in the job. While she was still in the process of sorting out her thoughts and accepting her life as it was while making the best out of it, her father said something to her that conveyed how disappointed *he* was at her not going ahead with her career. She was very upset with him for having hurt her ego thus. The very next morning she hurt her right hand's index finger badly by accidentally crushing it in a drawer while closing it. If she were at peace with herself and clear about her priorities and decisions, her father's expectations of her or his disappointment in her wouldn't have hurt her and she wouldn't have invited this injury to the index finger, which represents our ego.

Similarly, my husband was inviting one injury after another

to his ankles when he was expecting to hear the news of his routine transfer from a posting where he had achieved a lot of success in his work and was keen on accomplishing some more improvements in his department before the move. Feet and legs represent motion in life. He was anxious about moving fast in his work in order to finish it faster than he probably physically could. Interestingly, once he was made aware of this conflict within, he stopped inviting these injuries to himself.

This is how no injury comes to us uninvited.

Our genetics and our diet contribute a lot to our physical body. Yet, believing that we are bound to develop diabetes because our parents have it contributes in giving us the disease just as much as the genes do. Besides, we tend to follow most of the beliefs that we have grown up seeing our parents following. Some of those would have caused our parents to develop diabetes for themselves. Following those very negative belief patterns can also contribute to our developing the same disease. Being positive in our thoughts keeps us at peace and centred which also naturally attracts to us the diet that is most appropriate for our body's needs.

Sometimes, when we find it difficult to live in harmony with someone close to us, we develop a problem of acidity in our digestive system. What we eat matters a lot in deciding the state of our physical health but our thoughts play an important role in soothing or aggravating the symptoms in our physical body.

Pain often comes from lack of love in life. A deep desire to experience pure love causes pains in our physical body. A desire to be held, which is a physical reassurance of being loved gives rise to aches in the body.

Our back represents our support system. It supports our physical body to be erect. It is, therefore, affected by all the support related beliefs we carry. I have found financial support related insecurities to be very common amongst people and this probably is the reason lower back problems are becoming so common these days. So we can see that again it is the expectations, insecurities, guilt, blame, etc. that are the reasons for our physical sufferings too.

Such examples are endless and the topic deserves much more than the scope of this book permits. Here the idea is to point out that even our physical well-being is our choice. The strategy remains the same: being aware of our power packets!

SECTION V

EMPOWER YOUR ASPIRATION

Chapter 20

FOLLOW YOUR HIGHEST ASPIRATION

What is my highest aspiration?

By the highest aspiration I mean that which gives us supreme satisfaction. Our higher self had an objective it wanted to achieve when it decided to send us to the parents it did to and put us in the environment we grew up in. We are provided with all that is required for us to achieve that objective, because (as we have seen earlier) we are all-powerful and our higher self, together with the Creator, is creating for us all that is best for us in order to reach where it wants us to. If we would live with complete surrender to the Almighty, we would be able to see the opportunities being presented before us. If we consciously choose to believe, because of what we see around us or what we hear from others, that something else is better for us, we might actually be shutting up our ears to our own inner voice. Following that will ultimately lead to stress.

When we decide to use our power to change the stressful

situations around us for the better, we often tend to fall back on the same old patterns of negative thinking and again start focussing on the negativity around us that was created as a result of our negative thinking. This should not be treated as our failure. At such times, we need to look into our age-old beliefs like 'change takes time', because we deserve to experience instantaneous changes in our lives that are for our betterment. We also need to check our thought patterns and review the event patterns of our lives to see if we believe in our worthiness for success in whatever we take up.

Focussing on the negativity around us that we want to eliminate from our lives, will give it energy and only increase it in our lives further. We, therefore, need to start focussing on how we want to see our lives and what we want to see around us.

When we take it up to eliminate what is undesirable in our lives, it helps to ponder over what gives us the highest satisfaction. Is there so much stress in our lives because we are unable to do that which gives us the utmost joy? If so, what is it that has kept us from doing what gives us the supreme satisfaction? What is it that gives us the utmost joy? It could be different things for different individuals. It could be creating wealth for one; providing love, support and nurturing to one's family for another; doing a particular kind of social work for someone else. There are lessons to be learnt in each field. Different souls need to learn different lessons at different stages of their evolution. Comparing ourselves with others can distract us from the path our soul wants us to follow. Working towards our highest aspiration will never stress us because then we will consciously be doing what is in tune with our higher self's objective.

When we send out a question to the Universe, we are always

presented with an answer to it, in some form or the other. Therefore, once we acknowledge our desire to know what it is that our higher self aspires for the most, we will get an answer for sure. In fact, it is that inner voice we had been ignoring all this while, as we were busy looking at our lives from others' eyes and from the perspective of the rest of the world. What is best for another person might not be the best for us and vice versa. Each one of us is in our own individual journey. All of us have traversed different paths and have different lessons to learn. It is following our own inner voice that will ultimately lead us to internal peace and harmony because then we will be doing what is in tune with our essence — our soul!

Chapter 21

A WORD OF CAUTION!

Having read the book and understood it well, you are likely to feel motivated and empowered to change your life for the better and it is 100 per cent possible to do so. The new matter you have recently absorbed, though, is likely to wane off from your minds in a few days' time. You are then likely to fall back to your old patterns of thinking, simply because of the conditioning you have had for so many years. You have thought, spoken and acted in those old ways over and over again innumerable times in the past.

Besides, when you see, hear and feel the same things around you that were giving you stress earlier, you are likely to get too bogged down by the reality of your life to make enough efforts at changing it.

It is important to remember that the *reality* of your life that is so bothersome for you is what you have created for yourself. It is because it stresses you that you have decided to bring about a change in your life. So if you keep giving energy to what has been created already, you are continuing to waste, rather misuse, your power packets. Accept that it is you who has created that for yourself and with a better understanding of yourself and your life, go ahead and change your thought patterns, and hence your life and its situations. Give energy to the new positive beliefs in you and to the kind of life you want to experience, rather than to what has been troubling you so far. It is important to believe in yourself and that you deserve a better life, the type you dream of.

Once you realise and acknowledge your own power to create your life, it is easy and effortless to create it the way you wish. Initially, though, you need to keep reminding yourself to watch your thought patterns and keep correcting them. Don't curb the negative thoughts; watch as they come and understand their reason. Remember that the reason for all your suffering lies within, and this is such an empowering fact! It really means that you simply have to work on your own self to get rid of all the miseries in your life!

When we find ourselves amidst a situation that we don't want to be in, we believe that since the situation involves many other people, the only way out for us is to run away from it. If, anyway, we have to live it we do so grumbling and complaining about it. If we run away from it, we carry with ourselves the potential to create a similar situation again. So the need is to change our attitude. This seems difficult for some of us to do. Ego is a false protective covering that we create around ourselves when we are distant from our true selves. This ego doesn't allow anything that our conscious mind doesn't like to penetrate through to us. We refuse to accept that we could in any way be responsible for any negativity around or even inside us. We are unable to accept that there could be anything *inside* us that needs to be changed in order to improve our lives.

The concept of looking inside us to change our attitudes/

beliefs is not against that of unconditional love and acceptance for ourselves. Unconditional love and acceptance for ourselves doesn't stop us from watching our thoughts to determine which ones are negative and need to be changed in order to create a different environment for us to live in. The beliefs that we carry at the subconscious level are beyond the reach of our conscious mind, unless we live in a state of self-realisation. They come from our own past experiences, many of which we don't remember now. It might have appeared right for us to adopt those beliefs at a certain stage of our evolution. Now, if they are creating unpleasant environment for us, it will only help us if we identify, acknowledge and correct them.

I have come across people who believe they are the best (which is a very positive belief) because over the years they have tried to manage each situation in their lives intelligently and efficiently. They find it difficult to understand that they, in any way, could be responsible for the things that are giving them misery. They believe it is the other people who are wrong and are making them suffer. No matter how much I tried explaining them how I myself and many others that I know have experienced a change in their lives by bringing about a change in ourselves rather than wasting energies on blaming others, they were not very receptive to the idea. Such souls are not yet ready to shed their baggage and probably haven't yet learnt their lessons essential for them to evolve. We have to suffer to grow and evolve only as long as we believe so.

At times the reason is that the suffering is serving the person in some way. For example, a woman might be receiving her husband's attention, that she so craves for, only when she is unwell. Her soul will not allow her to get completely healthy. I know of a lady who wouldn't heal because she had nothing in her life to look forward to, nothing that would give her the drive to go on.

In order to be able to change your life and eliminate the unwanted from it, it is necessary to be keen for it. Begin with just one aspect of your life where you are dissatisfied. Bringing about a change in that area of your life will give you confidence to bring about a bigger change that you want, easily. Start by giving yourself some time in solitude, when you simply are with yourself and watch your thoughts related to that issue. Remember always, that you are a beautiful creation of the Creator and that all the cosmic energies move to your commands. Accept yourself the way you are and love yourself unconditionally till you are full of love. That really is your natural state of being.

SECTION VI

ENHANCE YOUR POWER

Chapter 22

RE-CREATING LIFE

The process of re-creating our lives can be structured in five steps:

- **Acceptance of the Existing Reality:** We have discussed this in detail earlier in the book. The reality that exists, even if undesirable, has been created by us for some reason and it is there for real. Let us simply accept it as the reality of that moment. By doing so, we are *not* resigning to our fate. We are only denying it the power to make us miserable.
- **Belief in the Creator:** This refers to not only our belief in the existence of the omnipotent, omnipresent but also in the fact that this universal energy source works to give us exactly what we wish for.
- **Clarity of Intent and Shifting our Focus:** Our energies are constantly communicating with the universal energies. Each thought that leaves us is energy of a particular frequency and on reaching the Creator, gets translated into a physical reality in our lives. Therefore, confused

thoughts bring back confusion in our lives. Conflicting thoughts create conflicting situations for us. We need to put in our efforts in clearly defining our desires so that we can easily manifest them.

Having clearly defined the reality that we want to create, let us make the conscious effort to shift our focus from the unwanted to the wanted. Our awareness tends to keep shifting to the reality that we don't like. We complain about it, pity ourselves for being in it and make sure the whole world knows about it. By doing so, we only keep empowering the situation to cause us to suffer.

By focusing on the reality we would like to be in, *that* is what we will energise.

- **Belief in our worthiness for what we Desire:** However much unbelievable it might sound, we often keep our desires from manifesting in our lives simply because we doubt our worthiness for the same. For example, we might crave for comfortably progressing further in our lives but our belief, "Success comes through struggle" will always keep us in situations where we do succeed and grow in life, but only through struggle. We need to become aware of such beliefs that we carry.
- **Surrender:** Being clear about the reality that we want to create, we need to let go of that desire, trusting the universe to work for us on it.

Chapter 23

SIMPLICITY

Exhausted from dealing with and sorting out the complications of our lives, there comes a day when we realise that life really is meant to be simple. It takes time, experience and wisdom to understand that life truly is all about simplicity.

Negativities that we have accumulated in and around us have complicated our lives and our thought processes. As a result, we begin to feel that it is a rare feat only a few are capable of, to connect with the Creator and reclaim our own inner power.

The fact is that each one of us is a spark of that brightest one. The Creator resides right within us. Why would a complicated or difficult process actually be required to lead us to our own core? All we need is the keenness to connect within and the belief that we deserve to.

Over the years, my experiences in healing have been focused on my cleansing and evolution. I have been fortunate to have had the opportunity to help numerous other people as a part of my healing journey as well. These experiences have taught me that the process of connecting with the Creator, seeking His help and receiving it instantly is simple and instantaneous. It makes our lives simpler, takes us closer to our Creator and teaches us to live each moment of our lives in His awareness.

In the following chapters, I have described some very simple techniques that can be used by anyone to heal his life on a daily basis.

Chapter 24

CLAIR SENSES

Everyone is born with Clair senses. In our culture, we are continuously programmed not to use our Clair senses and, instead, to rely heavily on the five commonly known senses of sight, smell, sound, speech and touch. While the latter help us to connect with the outer world around us, the former are our means of communicating with the Divine. As a result of this conditioning by the society, to one degree or another, most of us lose awareness of our Clair senses. The abilities, however, lie dormant in us.

Becoming aware of them and beginning to use them again is the only way to redevelop them.

When you are seeking the Creator's guidance, it might come to you in one of the following ways.

- **Clairvoyance:** Clairvoyance is the ability to see things that are not within normal vision. One receives the messages in the form of images/visuals in the inner eye or the third eye. Generally people who have an eye for visual details in the outside world tend to receive their messages clairvoyantly.

- **Clairaudience:** Clairaudience is the ability to hear things that the normal ear can't hear. You hear the messages in your inner ear. Those who are good listeners in the outer world are more likely to receive their messages from the Divine using their gift of clairaudience.
- **Clairsentience:** This is also called 'gut feeling' and most of us use it in our daily lives. You just 'feel' something is right or something is not. You can feel the message in your gut. Almost all of us have clairsentience active in us.
- **Claircognisance:** Sometimes you just 'know' about something or 'know' the right thing to do. Using this gift, you receive the message as some knowledge or an idea.

Often we receive messages through more than one Clair senses. For example, we might receive a visual and relevant knowledge along with it. We might hear a brief message and instantly feel what it means to convey.

Energy sensitive people sometimes have some more Clair senses active in them such as Clairscent (the ability to smell scents, odours and aromas not bound by physical parameters), Clairpresence (the ability to sense the presence of entities, angels etc.), and so on. However, the four main Clair senses described here are enough for us to focus on in order to begin to receive divine messages.

Chapter 25

SILENCE

The conscious mind is forever occupied with its own chatter. Conflicting thoughts in our mind make us stressed. This, in turn, causes us to think harder, giving the conscious mind reason to further generate a denser web of thoughts to keep us engaged in. In this entire process, we only end up increasing our confusion and the stress. This keeps us from finding the solution to our confusion, which is nowhere but within us.

A powerful tool to connect with our own thought processes is to observe silence. Finding a few minutes in our daily routine to sit in solitude, preferably close to Nature, is ideal for unwinding ourselves and understanding the conflicts we carry within. The energies of Nature are higher than those in closed rooms and therefore helpful in this process of releasing our negativities. If it isn't feasible to sit in a lawn or near trees and grass, sitting outside in a balcony is good enough.

Start with taking your awareness to a recent concern. Let your thoughts just flow. Refrain from fighting or even judging them.

You might realise that you are concerned about the health of a loved one. If they have been unwell for a while, you would be concerned about the pain and suffering they are going through. A student might be anxious about her upcoming exams. A usual fear in this situation is of not being able to prepare/perform well.

Thus connecting with our thoughts helps us realise where we need to correct them. We ought to focus on sending our compassion to our ailing loved ones instead of sympathy and feelings of helplessness. Instead of energising their pain, visualising them getting healthy and surrendering this desire to the Creator while asking Him for whatever our loved ones need to feel healthy and peaceful will certainly affect them positively. Similarly, our determination to do our best while preparing for our exams and surrendering our desire to perform well in the same will give us the much needed energy to prepare for the exams well. Our thoughts should strengthen our self-confidence, not sabotage it.

Doing this exercise for a few minutes daily helps us get clarity about our thoughts and with some practice we are able to easily divert them in a constructive direction.

Chapter 26

WRITING

Writing down our thoughts is another powerful exercise that helps in sorting them out.

When we are too confused to understand our own thoughts, it not only leads to stress within but also stops us from taking the necessary steps simply because we are unable to see what exactly the best course of action is.

Start penning down your thoughts. Begin with the intention of simply bringing on paper all that is coming up in the mind. Do it without mentally editing the thoughts. Write each word just as it comes up. Once you feel you have nearly finished writing them down, bring in the intention of sorting them out and keep writing. Allow the thought process of sorting them out to be equally natural and free flowing.

When we are engaged in this process with complete surrender, this is the point where we sometimes connect with our inner wisdom. Then, reading a few hours later what we had written can be very surprising for us because it sometimes presents us with a perspective that was not there in our conscious mind earlier. It always brings clarity about our thoughts and might, at times, guide us to a solution we were looking for. Using the written material, we can also try and prioritise our issues. This makes it easier for us to deal with them one by one.

Research shows that writing deep thoughts and feelings about stressful events helps people heal.

Sometimes deep hurt or anguish makes us brood over the incident that caused it over and over again. The more we think about it, the more hurt we feel and this becomes a vicious circle. Soon we find ourselves completely engulfed in depressing thoughts. At such times as well, writing down our thoughts not only gives an expression and a vent to our feelings, but also is capable of pulling us out of the whirlpool of negative thoughts.

Chapter 27

MEDITATION

A white light meditation is being described here. This meditation, while being very simple, is profound enough to connect you with the universal energy source of all creation when done properly.

- Find a quiet room where you won't be disturbed. You can put on some soothing, instrumental music but it is not a must.
- Sit comfortably, feet flat on the floor, spine straight, hands in lap or on your legs.
- Start taking deep breaths. Inhale through the nose, and relax. Breathe out through the nose and relax even more. Feel the relaxation throughout your body.
- In your third eye (inner eye), look up at your Crown Chakra (top of your head). Visualise bright white light entering your Crown Chakra. This is the brightest white light you have ever seen. It is coming into your Crown Chakra in a wide beam. Your Crown Chakra is where your physical being connects with the Divine.

- The white light enters your body and fills up the inside of your head. It reaches the throat and fills up the throat region. Through the shoulders it goes down into your arms, right upto your finger tips. It slowly starts travelling down your spine, while lighting up the surrounding parts of the body as well. Each part of your body gets lit up and feels relaxed. The light reaches the tailbone and travels through your legs into the feet.
- Take this light along with your energy deep into Mother Earth. Connect with Mother Earth and bring her energy up into your feet. Bring your awareness up your legs, up the spine, in the center of your chest. This is where the Heart Chakra is. (Those familiar with the seven major chakras can use this meditation to align the chakras by telling the white light to spin each chakra into perfect health and harmony as it passes through each chakra while going down the spine. You can enhance the experience by visualising the colour of each chakra being brightened up as the white light cleanses each of them.)
- Center yourself in your Heart Chakra. You are now filled up with the divine white light completely. This light is the pure unconditional love of the Creator. Feeling this energy inside you, your heart swells up with love. You are now centered, connected with the Creator and divinely protected. Whenever you feel like, you can slowly open your eyes.

After you have done this a few times, you will find that you can do it very fast and achieve the state of peace and calm instantly.

Using this meditation, you can bring about powerful healings through the white light of the Creator using the technique described in the next chapter.

Chapter 28

TAKING CREATOR'S HELP

As a result of the events we experience, we develop beliefs. The beliefs we carry create situations for us in accordance with their own existence and the cycle continues till something happens to change a belief of ours.

For example, if a person X wants to show his potential to his boss who doesn't think much of him, he might work very hard for it. As a result, when he does receive recognition and praise for his talent, he is likely to develop a belief that he must work hard to prove himself or that he *has* to prove himself. This belief, in turn, will repeatedly put him in situations where people will not appreciate his capabilities until he puts in that extra bit to prove his potential.

Let us consider another example where another person Y finds himself in a situation where he has been misunderstood. He tries hard but is unable to improve the relationship that has been strained due to the misunderstanding. Out of helplessness or self-pity in this situation, he might develop the belief that nobody understands him or that people misunderstand him.

This belief is sure to continue to create situations for him thereafter where he will inevitably find himself being misunderstood.

This is how, bit by bit, we keep replacing within ourselves the Creator's perspective on life with our own perspective. This happens because when something happens that arouses negative emotions like anger, jealousy, shock or grief in us, we get de-centered. As such, our response to the situation is different from one coming from a neutral, objective perspective.

If we feel the need to prove ourselves, it indicates a lack of our belief in ourselves. Those who believe in themselves don't need to prove themselves as they naturally and effortlessly display their talent through their work. Since they accept themselves as being good and don't doubt it, everything they do projects self-confidence. Therefore, they naturally attract acceptance and acclaim from others without the need to prove their worthiness for it. This is how the Creator really means us to be.

Similarly, a lack of understanding about oneself and one's conflicting thoughts and desires will lead one to project the same in his relationships, personal or professional. Clarity about what we carry inside will project the confidence we have in ourselves, in our interactions with others and it is highly unlikely that the person will end up in a situation where he feels misunderstood.

Having become aware of such thought patterns, one can make an effort to change them at the conscious level but the conflict in life persists till the conflicting thoughts continue to exist in the subconscious. With perseverance, the conscious mind can change the stuff we carry in our subconscious. However, in the present times when the human evolution on the planet has hastened, higher energies are available to us to ease our move into the New Age.

When we realise an erroneous belief within ourselves that seems to be creating an undesirable pattern of situations in our life, we can then ask the Creator to intervene and break that pattern. Using a simple technique described here, we can now start replacing back our own perspective on various aspects of life with the Creator's perspective and understanding on the same. This, combined with our conscious effort at beginning to look at life differently, will change the patterns in our lives that have been making us miserable.

For this, we need to follow the simple three-step process described here.

- Identify the pattern in your life that you need to change. You might find it useful to take help of the 'Silence' and 'Writing' techniques described earlier, to get clarity about the aspect of your life that is causing you maximum suffering. If we take the example of the person X mentioned earlier, the help we need is in the following areas:
    - Lack of self-belief.
    - Having to repeatedly prove ourselves.
- Fully understand the process of the white light meditation described in the previous chapter. It might take practicing it a few times initially to get comfortable with the entire sequence of steps to follow while doing it. Once you are thorough with it, use it as follows.
    - Having centered yourself in the Heart Chakra, before opening the eyes, bring your awareness on the Creator who is ever-connected with you through your Crown Chakra in the form of the divine white light.

  - Mentally say: "Creator, I be downloaded with the Creator's understanding of believing in myself into each cell of my being. Thank you."
  - Wait till you feel your entire being has indeed received the download completely. Allow your intuition to guide you when it's over. With practice, it will happen in a few seconds.
  - Mentally say: "Creator, I be downloaded with the Creator's understanding of proving myself into each cell of my being. Thank you." Wait till the download feels complete.

- We were created with Creator's own light. It was in the process of various experiences we went through during our journey that we lost His perspective on things. Once lost, the wrong perspective kept creating negative experiences for us. It helps, therefore, to receive the following download from the Creator as well:
  - "Creator, I be downloaded with the Creator's understanding of what had happened when I first lost belief in myself, into each cell of my being. Thank you."
  - Wait till you feel the download is complete.

Without carrying out the third step as discussed here, it is likely that the download received in step two be lost again due to the memories held within the cells of the soul, of the event that had caused us to lose it in the first place. The download received in step three replaces those memories with the Creator's perspective on the event.

To provide a little more clarity on the process, I will take the person Y's example as well and illustrate the process again.

- Here, we need to have the Creator's knowledge about:
    - Having clarity about our thoughts.
    - Having clarity about our intentions.
    - Understanding ourselves.
- In the meditative state, having just done the white light meditation, before opening the eyes, mentally say:
    - "Creator, I be downloaded with the Creator's understanding of having clarity about my thoughts into each cell of my being. Thank you." Wait till you feel the download is complete.
    - "Creator, I be downloaded with the Creator's understanding of having clarity about my intentions into each cell of my being. Thank you." Wait till the download is complete.
    - "Creator, I be downloaded with the Creator's understanding of understanding myself into each cell of my being. Thank you." Wait till the download is complete.
- Further, mentally say: "Creator, I be downloaded with the Creator's understanding of what had happened when I was first misunderstood by others, into each cell of my being. Thank you."

Here we are asking for the Creator's perspective on what had happened when for the very first time we were misunderstood, because that is when we are likely to have lost confidence and clarity in our own thoughts and intentions. Erasing those memories and receiving the right downloads will bring us back on the right track.

These are two very simple examples I have used to illustrate how our thoughts get distorted and how we can now amend them taking help from the Creator. Amazingly simple and yet amazingly profound!

Life situations can be more complex than the examples we have considered. Besides, it is easier to analyse someone else's situation but rather difficult when we ourselves are in the middle of it. However, the processes of silence and writing can be of immense help in bringing us clarity about our life situations.

Even though our energy changes the instant we receive these downloads, it takes some time for them to manifest into physical realities in our lives just as our earlier distorted beliefs had been manifesting themselves in the form of undesirable situations. Things around us change in a very subtle manner. It is only when we assess the situation after a few weeks have elapsed that we are able to gauge the difference.

There is another dimension of this technique. It involves using and trusting our Clair senses.

Let us now consider two persons A and B. Of late, A has somehow ended up feeling humiliated by B repeatedly. A now wants to change this pattern. He can do so by taking help from the Creator in the following manner:

- Center yourself using the white light meditation. In the end, before opening the eyes take your awareness to your connection with the Creator which is in your Crown Chakra and mentally ask: "Creator, help me to understand the reason within me that brings me humiliation through B. Thank you."

  Having sent out this question, it is very important to mentally relax and trust that you will receive the answer. The answer might come to you in the form of a sentence, a visual, some feeling, some knowledge or a combination of one or more of these. The only thing that can stop you from receiving the answer is your anxiety, your doubts regarding the possibility of such an event or your doubts regarding your worthiness for receiving an answer you seek from the universe.

- The answer you receive will be in a manner that you can best understand. Let us assume that you hear/see/feel /get to know that in some previous lifetime you (A) were B's boss and had caused him humiliation. Sometimes you respond to a situation in a certain manner but later feel guilty for your action. Then the soul decides to pay back the other soul involved, by suffering in some manner similar to the manner it had caused the other one to suffer.
- Having understood life better, you are now ready to learn your lesson peacefully and painlessly. You can now surrender the guilt the soul carries and stop paying for it in the future. Once you can receive the Creator's understanding on the event that gave you the guilt, it becomes natural to forgive yourself and move on from the situation as one of the contracts that bonded the two souls through Karma would have been removed from the soul. You have to mentally say: "Creator, I be downloaded with the Creator's understanding of what had happened when I caused humiliation to B. Thank you." Wait till the downloading is complete.

  Then mentally say: "Creator, I be downloaded with Creator's understanding of forgiving myself. Thank you"

Once we download ourselves with the Creator's understanding of forgiving ourselves, it completes the process of dropping the guilt as we realise that whatever happened, happened for a reason in the past. We are then ready to move on from the situation. Similarly, once we download ourselves with the Creator's understanding about proving ourselves, it becomes natural for us to understand that we really are not meant to prove ourselves to anyone but just believe in ourselves.

Even if the process seems a bit complicated initially, begin with giving yourself downloads of Creator's understanding of simple concepts like loving ourselves, accepting ourselves unconditionally, accepting change, etc. Once we start cleansing ourselves energetically on a regular basis using this technique, we slowly begin to realise the pleasant changes that start creeping into ourselves and our lives. It brings more clarity about our lives and about the changes we want to see in our lives. This clarity, in turn, helps us cleanse ourselves using the process described here.

Chapter 29

SOME USEFUL DOWNLOADS

Each one's life is different. The situations and miseries experienced by each one of us are different. We can always use our Clair senses to seek help from the Divine in solving our problems. Yet, there are some common patterns of sufferings and negative emotions that most of us experience. Following are some downloads all of us could benefit from, irrespective of the kind of concerns we have in our lives. Even if we don't require a particular download, receiving some additional energy from the Creator can never harm.

- Connection with the Creator, Creator's understanding of:
    - Creator's unconditional love.
    - My worthiness for the Creator's unconditional love.
    - Being connected with the Creator.
    - My connection with the Creator.

    - Receiving messages from the Divine.
    - My worthiness to receive messages from the Divine.
- Unconditional acceptance of the moment, Creator's understanding of:
    - Unconditionally accepting what comes.
    - Being present in the moment.
- Resistance to change, Creator's understanding of:
    - Change.
    - Accepting change.
- Loving, accepting and forgiving the self, Creator's understanding of:
    - Loving.
    - Being loved.
    - Loving myself.
    - Liking myself.
    - Being accepted.
    - Accepting myself unconditionally.
    - Forgiving.
    - Forgiving myself.
- Surrendering to the Creator, Creator's understanding of surrendering to the Creator:
    - Trusting.
    - Trusting myself.

- Material abundance, Creator's understanding of:
    - Money.
    - Wealth.
    - Material abundance.
- Some general concepts, Creator's understanding of:
    - Expectations.
    - Perfection.
    - Being perfect.
    - Judging.
    - Being judged.
    - Relaxing.
    - What I want.
    - My worthiness to get what I want.
    - Valuing myself for what I am.
    - Being valued for what I am.
    - Controlling.
    - Being controlled.
    - Struggling.
    - Evolving without having to struggle.
    - Jealousy.
    - Support.
    - Resentment.

  - Living without resenting.
  - Being happy.
  - Being supported by the Creator.
  - Expressing myself.

When the soul develops guilt for something, it continues to pay for it till a certain point comes when it has suffered enough in paying or something teaches it to forgive itself. Till then, it is unable to forgive itself probably because it feels if it does so, it might commit the same mistake again. Then it becomes necessary for us to ask for the download of the Creator's understanding of what had happened when it was unsafe for us to forgive ourselves. Similarly, if at some time we did surrender our desire to the Creator but it didn't manifest due to some other negative beliefs that we were carrying, we might have developed the belief that it is unsafe to surrender to the Creator. To erase those memories of the soul, we can further ask for the following downloads:

- Creator's understanding of what had happened when:
  - It was unsafe for me to forgive myself.
  - It was unsafe for me to surrender to the Creator.
  - Money was unsafe for me.
  - Money corrupted me.
  - I abused my wealth.
  - Change was unsafe for me.
  - It was unsafe for me to receive messages from the Divine.
  - I was unsupported.

- I had to struggle in order to grow and evolve.
- I was controlled.
- It was unsafe for me to express myself.
- It was unsafe for me to speak the truth.
- It was unsafe for me to trust.
- It was unsafe for me to trust myself, etc.

Using this technique in your day-to-day life, you can begin to achieve much deeper understanding of this work with experience. It is not advisable, however, to start giving these downloads to others without personal guidance.

MY JOURNEY AS A HEALER

My journey as a healer began when I started learning Reiki in order to be able to help my daughter feel better. She was suffering from asthma. As I began cleansing myself through Reiki, which was essential in order to become an effective Reiki channel, I started feeling wonderful. I started applying it to various day to-day issues in my life. The results were encouraging. I went on to complete my journey in Reiki by learning all levels of it including the Master level. While attuning a number of people to become Reiki channels, I also kept helping others get better by giving them Reiki on a regular basis. I will forever be grateful to my capable teacher Mrs Parinda Macwana for guiding me on this path.

As I was beginning to feel the peace inside me, I was also beginning to feel an urge to be able to help others find the same inside them. Around that time, a friend introduced me to Dr Sangeeta Sahi, who became my teacher and friendly guide on the path that I then followed. It was as if she helped me discover a hidden door inside me — opening which has led me to my hidden treasures. The work that I learnt from her was

'Theta Healing'. It has contributed a big deal in my personal progress.

This book encapsulates the knowledge I believe I have gained through my experiences over the past life times and have recently tapped into. Whatever our soul experiences and learns never leaves us. It appears as though we are beginning from scratch every time we take birth, but we spend very little time learning, actually remembering, what we have already learnt. Then we go on to experience new things necessary for our further evolution.

This journey thus began with my own healing and my efforts at finding peace within, which I did. My daughter, too, has been rid of asthma since long. The healing work that I do and teach now has emerged as an essence of all that I have learnt during my journey, which has helped me to rediscover myself. It has made me understand the fact that we are constituted of love, peace, joy and harmony. Everything else that we carry is external to us. As we begin to shed this undesirable baggage, we start living our lives in our natural state of happiness.

Each one of us is directly connected to the Creator. Various experiences that we go through however, create a baggage that our soul begins to carry. It is this baggage of negative belief patterns and certain unpleasant memories stored in our cells that slowly make us drift away from the Creator. In fact we even tend to drift away from our own higher self and start leading stressful lives. Through healing I find it natural to help an individual find his connection back with himself as well as the Creator of the Universe. The healing of an individual, though, is entirely dependent on the keenness of the soul to get rid of the baggage, and the urgency it feels to be healed. Those who seek healing and are keen on it are the ones who get healed.

It is an extremely gratifying experience to see people feel lighter through this work. May the power be with us.